# HIGHGATE

PAUL FEENEY

The History Press

*In memory of my mother*
*Mary (Mamie) Feeney (1922–1991)*

First published 2008

The History Press Ltd
The Mill, Brimscombe Port
Stroud, Gloucestershire, GL5 2QG
www.thehistorypress.co.uk

British Library Cataloguing in Publication Data.
A catalogue record for this book is available from the British Library.

ISBN 978 0 7509 5101 2

Typesetting and origination by The History Press Ltd.
Printed in Great Britain

# Contents

Highgate Archway, *c.* 1912.

# INTRODUCTION

Highgate began as a small thirteenth-century hillside hamlet on the edge of a large area of hunting grounds that formed part of the then Bishop of London's estate, just north of London. Early in the fourteenth century, the Bishop had a new road laid to improve the steep gravel track that had become a popular route through his land, to and from Islington Village and central London. The Bishop then erected a tollgate at the top of the hill to collect tolls from travellers using the new road, which meant that the Bishop now controlled the main northern route in and out of London. The original tollgate, removed in 1892, was situated next to where the Gatehouse pub now stands. This being the highest tollgate in London, it was generally identified as the High Gate, but early spellings of the name do vary from *Higate, Hyegate* and *Heighgate*. Later, two more tollgates were erected, one at the top of Dartmouth Park Hill and another next to where the Spaniards Inn now stands. In around 1813, a further tollgate was positioned at the foot of the newly-opened Archway Road. This whole area became known as Highgate.

Situated on the summit and slopes of one of the highest hills in the historical county of Middlesex, Highgate was renowned as a healthy place to live and, during the fifteenth century, the area attracted more and more people to settle there. The population continued to grow throughout the sixteenth and seventeenth centuries, with many aristocrats moving to Highgate and building some very grand houses. In the eighteenth and nineteenth centuries, a lot of professionals, merchants and entrepreneurs came to live in the area

The tollgate at the foot of Archway Road (removed in 1876).

and they too made their mark on the local architecture with their very elegant residences. These wealthy nobles and businessmen cemented the foundations of Highgate's enduring character, with many of their beautiful buildings still to be found gracing the older streets of Highgate. Indeed, Highgate has more than a hundred English Heritage listed buildings, which, surprisingly, include some entrance gates, garden walls, milestones and the odd red telephone box.

As with all areas of London, throughout the centuries Highgate has seen a good deal of poverty, but the Highgate of today is very much an up-market community, sandwiched between vast areas of green parks and woodlands.

Inconsiderately and bizarrely, Highgate is now divided between the three London boroughs of Haringey, Camden and Islington. The increased population and high volumes of traffic have transformed the old calm of Highgate into a more bustling environment of modern living. As always, its higher elevations continue to afford great views over Hampstead Heath and across Greater London as far as the Surrey Hills to the south. In recent decades, Highgate's pricey properties have mainly attracted the more affluent home buyers, and it has become a popular place of residence for many well-known celebrities. The eighteenth and nineteenth-century resident poets, artists and thespians would have rented rooms in Highgate; whereas today's equivalents can afford to buy and maintain the most expensive houses.

The illustrations within this book have mainly been taken from my own collection of late nineteenth and early twentieth-century picture postcards, photographs, drawings, engravings and other printed and hand-written ephemera of Highgate and the surrounding areas. In pictures of street scenes, people may often appear to be posing; this is because in early photography people had to stand perfectly still to allow for the long film exposure times. Hence, when someone moved while the camera shutter was open it caused the image on the film to be blurred in the direction of the motion.

Most of the illustrations show Highgate as it was around 100 years ago, and these are accompanied by brief early histories of famous people, places, buildings and events that have helped to take this thirteenth-century remote hamlet, in the highest part of North London, through its journey to become one of London's most prominent and popular places to live.

I hope this book will take you on a pleasant journey through Highgate's past, and that it will remain on your bookshelf for future reference to this special place called Highgate.

*Paul Feeney*

# ACKNOWLEDGEMENTS

With just a few exceptions, the illustrations in this book come from my own collection and I believe that the original copyrights on the old images have now expired, but I would like to acknowledge and thank all of the photographers, artists and publishers that created these wonderful images for us to look back on. I have taken all reasonable care to avoid any copyright infringements, but should any valid issue arise, then I will look to correct it in subsequent editions.

Special thanks to Mary Embleton and Nicole Thorn of Channing School for providing me with and permitting me to use the pictures on pages 36 (bottom), 37 (top) and 44, and to Nick Ellis of Prickett & Ellis for providing me with and permitting me to use the pictures on pages 48 (top) and 88 (top and bottom).

I am grateful to every Highgate historian that has ever written a book or made contributions to relevant Internet pages, thus enabling me to research the subject area and to double check facts relating to my own knowledge of the neighbourhood. In particular, I acknowledge the books by historians John Richardson, Sydney Kitchener, Joan Schwitzer, Ken Gay and nineteenth-century writers Frederick Prickett, John H. Lloyd and Edward Walford.

View of Highgate Village from an original nineteenth-century steel engraving entitled 'Gate House, Highgate' which appeared in the book *Views of London, Westminster, and their Vicinities,* illustrated by John Woods and first published in 1838.

# MAP OF HIGHGATE

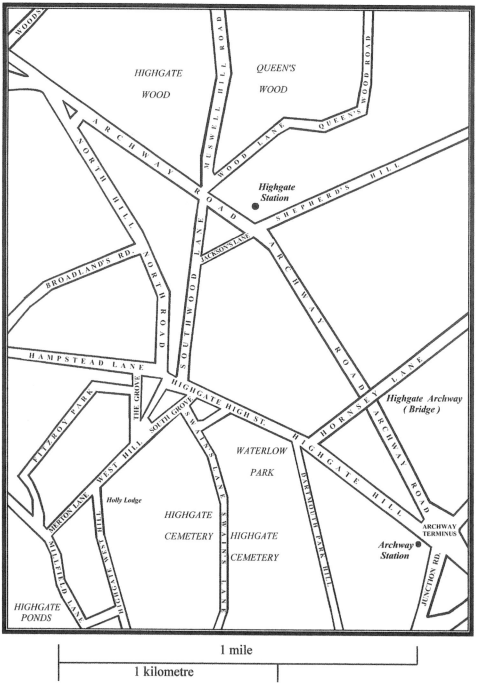

WOODS

HIGHGATE WOOD

QUEEN'S WOOD

MUSWELL HILL ROAD

QUEEN'S WOOD ROAD

WOOD LANE

ARCHWAY ROAD

NORTH HILL

SHEPHERD'S HILL

Highgate Station

BROADLAND'S RD.

NORTH ROAD

JACKSON'S LANE

SOUTHWOOD LANE

ARCHWAY ROAD

HAMPSTEAD LANE

THE GROVE

HIGHGATE HIGH ST.

HORNSEY LANE

Highgate Archway
( Bridge )

FITZROY PARK

SOUTH GROVE

SWAIN'S LANE

WATERLOW

PARK

HIGHGATE HILL

ARCHWAY ROAD

WEST HILL

Holly Lodge

HIGHGATE
CEMETERY

SWAIN'S LANE

HIGHGATE
CEMETERY

DARTMOUTH PARK HILL

ARCHWAY
TERMINUS

MERTON LANE

HIGHGATE WEST HILL

MILLFIELD LANE

Archway
Station

JUNCTION RD.

HIGHGATE
PONDS

1 mile

1 kilometre

*Approximate Scale.*

# 1

# *(Lower) Highgate Hill*

The Archway tram terminus at the foot of Highgate Hill, *c.* 1930. The Archway Tavern, on the right of the picture, was rebuilt in 1886 and stands on the site of the original 1820s tavern. The Charing Cross, Euston & Hampstead Railway Co. opened the underground station, on the left of the picture, in 1907. It was originally called Highgate Station, and was successively renamed Archway (Highgate) in 1939, Highgate (Archway) in 1941, and Archway in 1947. The domes of St Joseph's Church can be seen up the hill in the distance. The tramlines on the right of the picture continue on up the Archway Road. Archway Station is now located underneath the Archway Tower, a bland 195ft office block which was completed in 1963.

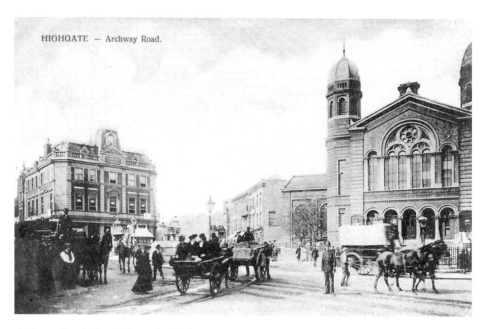

Archway Road viewed from the Archway tram terminus at the junction of Highgate Hill and Archway Road, *c.* 1904. To the right is the Archway Road Wesleyan Methodist Chapel.

*Archway Tavern.*                                                    *Highgate.*

The Archway Tavern, in the centre of the picture, separating Highgate Hill on the left, and Archway Road on the right, *c.* 1904. The tram terminus is just in front of the tavern. The Holborn Union Infirmary, opened in 1879 and now known as the Archway Campus, can be seen just behind the tavern.

Horse-drawn bus at the old Archway bus terminus, by unknown artist, *c.* 1872. In 1870, London's first horse-drawn tram service began. As with horse-drawn buses, some hills posed a problem for the horses and so cable haulage was employed, as on Highgate Hill.

Two trams make their way down Highgate Hill, *c.* 1905. The Highgate Hill Cable Tramway opened on 29 May 1884 and was the first cable tramway in Europe. The cable tramway ran from Archway, up Highgate Hill to a point along Southwood Lane. The cable tramway was closed in 1909 and reopened as an electric tramway in 1910.

Highgate Hill, as viewed from near the bottom of the hill and facing north, *c.* 1905. The Whittington Stone, outside John Palmer's Whittington Stone pub, has always attracted the attention of young children. The decorative railing and pillars to the right mark the Highgate Hill boundary of the old Holborn Union Infirmary (now Archway Campus). The dome of St Joseph's and the spire of the Cromwell Avenue Presbyterian Church can be seen in the distance.

Highgate Archway sometime in the 1820s, with the tollgate at the bottom of Archway Road, just this side of the Whittington Almshouses (College), on the right. The Archway Road tolls were abolished in 1876.

Whittington's Almshouses, Highgate, from an engraving, *c.* 1830. At the south end of Archway Road, to the east, were the Whittington Almshouses (known as Whittington College), erected here in about 1822 by the Mercers' Co. out of the Whittington Foundation. On the lawn in front there was a statue of Richard Whittington as a boy. The almshouses were each occupied by an elderly single woman. There was a resident clergyman, and a chapel where the almswomen were expected to worship. The picturesque buildings were pulled down in 1967 to make way for the widening of Archway Road. The Mercers' Co. then moved the almshouses to new premises in Felbridge, Surrey.

Whittington's Arms House, Archway Road, Highgate, drawn by Mr Shepherd, from an engraving by T. Dale, *c.* 1827. The travellers will have just passed through the Archway Road tollgate, which was to the right just down the hill.

The Whittington Stone, commemorating Richard Whittington's life and work, stands near to the roadside just 200yds (60m) up from the Archway underground station, on the west side of Highgate Hill.

# The Legend of Dick Whittington

The legend of Dick Whittington was first recorded in about 1605 and the story continued to grow throughout the seventeenth and eighteenth centuries. It appeared in many children's books and in the nineteenth century other characters were added and the story became the subject for pantomimes. New versions of the story are still being published, and the tale of Dick Whittington continues to be told in pantomimes today

The fairy tale of Dick Whittington and the cat that made his fortune are familiar to people all over the world but most have no knowledge of the real Richard Whittington. He was born sometime between 1350 and 1360 in Pauntley, Gloucestershire, the son of Sir William Whittington, Lord of the Manor. He was from an affluent family but being the younger son, he would not inherit his father's estate. Consequently, he was sent to London to earn his living as an apprentice to the Mercers' Co. in the City of London. He became a successful trader, dealing in valuable imports such as silks and velvets. He was also an exporter of wool and a moneylender. He later became a councilman, an alderman, a member of the Mercers' Co., and Lord Mayor of London in 1397. He was reported to have lent large sums of money to both King Richard II and his successor, Henry IV.

He married Alice Fitzwarren in 1402. He was elected Mayor for the second time in 1406, and for the third time in 1419. He also became a Member of Parliament and sat as a judge. He was even employed by Henry V to supervise the expenditure on Westminster Abbey. Richard Whittington donated much of his profits to the city. He financed many things, including the rebuilding of the Guildhall, a ward for unmarried mothers at St Thomas' Hospital, and drainage systems for areas around Billingsgate and Cripplegate. When he died in 1423, he left in his will £7,000 to charity, which, in those days, was a very large sum of money. Some of this money was used to rebuild Newgate Prison, repair St Bartholomew's Hospital, build the Whittington Almshouses, build the first library in Guildhall and install some of the first public drinking fountains. The Whittington Charity still exists and disburses money through the Mercers' Co. The Whittington Hospital on Highgate Hill was named after him and their logo features the legendary Whittington cat.

Street urchins congregate around the Whittington Stone on Highgate Hill, *c.* 1902. Note the young boy to the left of the stone wearing a mortarboard, which were often worn by young choristers in about 1900.

The Whittington Stone outside John Palmer's Whittington Stone public house (built around 1860) on Highgate Hill, c. 1902. The stone marks the spot where Dick Whittington was reputed to have heard the sound of Bow bells peeling 'turn again Whittington'. The original stone was repaired and replaced many times before the present stone was constructed in 1854. This stone has also been repaired several times over the years, and a cat was added to the top of the stone in 1964.

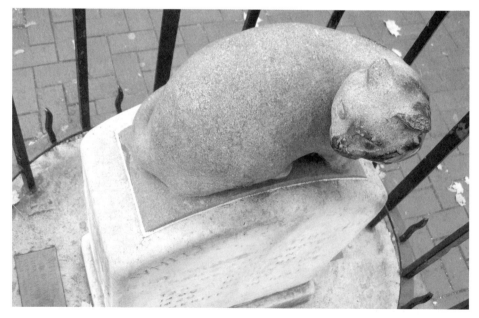

The Whittington Stone with cat, c. 2008. The sculpture of Dick Whittington's cat was added to the top of the stone in 1964. The cat is posed in a typical feline crouched position looking warily back over its shoulder and down the hill towards the City of London below.

The new main entrance to Whittington Hospital in Magdala Avenue, *c.* 2008. The hospital is located at the lower end of Highgate Hill, about 270yds (247m) from the Archway underground station. It stretches as far as Dartmouth Park Hill to the west, covering land that has provided medical services, in various guises, since 1473.

St Pancras Infirmary, seen here in about 1904, was built in 1870 and is situated between Dartmouth Park Hill and Swains Lane, bordering the southern edge of Waterlow Park. It was originally the infirmary for the poor people of St Pancras parish. It was later called Highgate Hospital and subsequently became part of the Highgate Wing of Whittington Hospital on Dartmouth Park Hill.

Holborn Union Infirmary, aerial view, *c.* 1920. Whittington College is just across Archway Road to the right of the picture, and the Archway Tavern can be seen bottom right of the picture. The Holborn Union Infirmary opened in 1879 on the east side of Highgate Hill. It covered the area within the boundaries of Highgate Hill, Despard Road, Lidyard Road and Archway Road. It later became Archway Hospital, and in 1948 it became part of the Whittington Hospital and known as the Archway Wing. Fifty years later, in 1998, it was sold by the NHS and jointly purchased by Middlesex University and University College London. It has since been renamed the Archway Campus.

East entrance of Islington Infirmary, Highgate Hill, *c.* 1905. The Infirmary was an 800-bed poor people's infirmary, built by Islington Guardians in about 1900, alongside the old Smallpox Hospital's buildings, which were then converted for use as staff accommodation. In 1930, the Infirmary became Islington (St Mary's) Hospital and with the arrival of the National Health Service in 1948, it combined with St Pancras and Holborn Union to become Whittington Hospital.

# 2

# *Top of Highgate Hill*

Hornsey Lane, *c.* 1905. Several grand houses were built along the whole length of the newly-fashionable Hornsey Lane in the latter part of the nineteenth century. This was a popular area for boarding schools during the nineteenth and early twentieth centuries. It is said that Michael Faraday, the famous nineteenth-century chemist and physicist, regularly stayed in Highgate at a house that is believed to have been in Tile Kiln Lane, off Hornsey Lane. Michael Faraday was interred in the Sandemanian (Christian sect of which Faraday was a member) plot in Highgate Cemetery, when he died in 1867.

Wynnstay, situated at the Hornsey end of Hornsey Lane, opposite the junction of Sunnyside Road, *c.* 1905. An Edwardian lady stands on the front step holding a parasol to shade herself from the sun. During the late nineteenth and early twentieth century the house was used as a girls' private day and boarding school.

Number 100 Hornsey Lane, *c.* 1905. This is one of the many grand houses that were built along Hornsey Lane in the late nineteenth century.

Highgate Presbyterian Church, on the corner of Cromwell Avenue and Hornsey Lane, *c.* 1908. It was built in 1887, just a year after the founding of the Presbyterian Church of England, chiefly by Scottish immigrants. In 1967, its name was changed to the Highgate United Reform Church. The church spire was removed following bomb damage in the Second World War. The building was converted into residential flats in the late 1970s and is now known as Cloisters Court.

The Revd Alexander Ramsay B.D., pictured around 1899, was the minister at Highgate Presbyterian Church, Cromwell Avenue from 1889–1922.

View from Archway, St. Aloysius' College, Highgate N.

St Aloysius' College, Hornsey Lane, *c.* 1910. The Brothers of Our Lady of Mercy founded the College as a private Roman Catholic secondary school for boys in 1879. It was built on the site of an eighteenth-century house called Belle Vue, which itself had been used as a school on at least two occasions during the early part of the nineteenth century. When it first opened, the headmaster, Brother Desiderius, placed an advert in the *Universe*, Britain's biggest selling Catholic newspaper, announcing that the new establishment was for the benefit of 'respectable boys of middle class'. Catholic boys of the upper class had been catered for from the early nineteenth century by Catholic public schools, but now London was to have its own 'middle class' boarding college that would teach a wide range of academic subjects, including the classics, mensuration (the science of measurement), book-keeping, civics, divinity (the study of religion), French, Latin and German. There would also be a wide range of sporting activities.

Hornsey Lane was still quite rural in the early years of the school. Those two major Highgate landmarks of St Joseph's Retreat and the new Archway Bridge were not even on the drawing board at that stage! The imposing school building stood in a prominently high position, fronting Hornsey Lane and near to the edge of the old bridge, high above Archway Road.

Rear view of St Aloysius' College, taken from the orchard, with the dome of St Joseph's in the background, *c.* 1906.

Saturday afternoon walk for the borders of St Aloysius' College, through the village and past the Old Gate House. This illustration is from the second issue of the college magazine, April 1891.

St Aloysius' College, viewed from the playground at the rear, *c.* 1911. In 1911, a new building was constructed at the back west side of the main building, doubling the school's capacity. In addition to extra classrooms, the new building provided much-needed science laboratories, a gymnasium/assembly hall, and a roof terrace. The two buildings now formed an L-shape that ran along Hornsey Lane and down the western edge of the playground at the rear. Connecting doors on the first floor linked the two buildings; otherwise access to the new building was via the playground on the lower ground level, and the old building's terrace on the upper ground level. All of the trees along the west side of the playground were removed to accommodate the new building. Most of the windows on this side of the school provided magnificent hilltop views across London to the south. Apart from the tree in the middle of the playground, this view remained unchanged through to 1972 when the main building fronting Hornsey Lane was demolished.

The College was well known for its sporting achievements, particularly football. In 1929, the Aloysians won the London Schools League Championship and the London Old Boys' Cup. The College was also renowned for its music and amateur dramatics. The Aloysian Association and the Old Aloysian Dramatics Society were formed in 1914 and held concerts and dances in the College Hall; these continued throughout the twentieth century.

In 1940, following the start of the Second World War, all the pupils were evacuated out of London to Stainsby Hall, in Derby, where they continued with their education. The British Army commandeered the school buildings in Hornsey Lane for the duration of the war. During the war, enemy bombers hit the main building, and the school chapel and central staircase were damaged. The pupils returned to the school after the war, but from 1945 the college would only admit day pupils and no new boarders taken in. In 1950, the school relinquished its independent character and became a voluntary-aided grammar school. In 1961, the Brothers of Mercy handed over to the De La Salle Brothers and withdrew from the school. In the late 1960s, the then Labour government introduced plans for the phasing out of grammar schools and replacing them and secondary moderns with a comprehensive system. In 1971, St Aloysius' College surrendered its grammar school status and became a comprehensive school. Within a year, the original old school building that fronted Hornsey Lane was demolished and a new school block was built near to the bottom of the old school playground.

St Aloysius' College, as viewed from the gardens at the rear of the main Hornsey Lane building, *c.* 1905. Everything in this picture is now long gone, demolished in about 1972 to make way for characterless concrete and glass Lego style school blocks, new playgrounds and staff car parks.

St Aloysius' College, Champions, North London Secondary Schools, *c.* 1917. Many Old Aloysians, went on to achieve great success in a wide variety of professions, and some of these professions serve to highlight the school's historical fondness of drama, religion, and sport.

Famous old Aloysians include: Gary Breen, professional footballer, Premier League and Irish International; Joe Cole, professional footballer, Premier League, England International; John Crowley, Catholic Bishop of Middlesbrough; Sir Michael Gambon CBE, award-winning actor; Danny Granville, professional footballer, Premier League and Championship; James Herbert, best selling author; Malcolm McMahon, Catholic Bishop of Nottingham; Peter Sellers CBE, comedian, award-winning actor, writer and film director; and George Stack, Catholic Bishop, Auxiliary Bishop of Westminster.

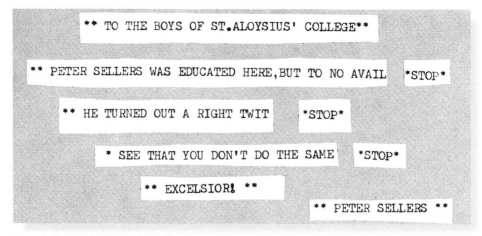

Peter Sellers took a break from filming in the USA to send this cable to the boys of St Aloysius' College to mark the school's centenary in 1979.

St. Joseph's Retreat, Highgate

St Joseph's Church and Retreat on Highgate Hill viewed from Waterlow Park, *c.* 1910. St Joseph's is a well-known North London landmark. The copper dome, with a patina of green, is 130ft above the level of the cross of St Paul's and can be seen from far across London. The church and retreat were established in about 1858 by Father Ignatius Spencer (whose descendants would include Winston Churchill and Diana, Princess of Wales), at a time when the relaxation of legal control over Catholicism was taking place.

St Joseph's Roman Catholic Church, Highgate Hill, *c.* 1905. An English Heritage Grade II listed building, the church is 146ft long and more than 55ft wide. The ceiling is 53ft high from floor to internal apex. The dome is estimated to weigh, with its supporting brickwork, 2,000 tons.

*Above:* St Joseph's Church interior, *c.* 1912. In 1858, the Passionist Fathers from Hendon, led by Father Ignatius Spencer, bought the former Black Dog Tavern on Highgate Hill. They converted its ground floor into the chapel of St Joseph, with accommodation upstairs for a community of eighteen. In 1861, a purpose-built church replaced the original chapel, but even this became too small and so the work of building the current St Joseph's commenced on 24 May 1888. The enthusiastic Brother Alphonsus Zeegers, working in habit and stonemason's apron, oversaw the construction. The present church opened its doors to a huge congregation on 22 November 1889 and, for many days afterwards, enormous crowds of people poured in to see the ornate Italian interior and the legendary dome.

The High Altar with canopy, St Joseph's Church, Highgate, *c.* 1908. The church contains many historical features within its Italian interior, including the canopy over the high altar, the Sicilian marble altar piece, the cylindrical steel safe of the tabernacle from the 1861 church, the mosaic pavement in the sanctuary and the hand-painted vaulted ceiling that was painted by Nathaniel Westlake in 1891. The church is also the proud possessor of an organ built by the famous organ builder, William Hill.

*Opposite, bottom:* This drawing from about 1884 shows the view opposite St Joseph's Retreat looking up Highgate Hill. The drawing depicts Crown Cottages with the Old Crown Inn and tea gardens just beyond them and a water cart settling the dust on Highgate Hill. Crown Cottages have long since been demolished and a car park now occupies the site.

Highgate Hill, looking south, with the Old Crown public house on the left at the junction with Hornsey Lane, and St Joseph's Church and Retreat on the right, *c.* 1904.

# Highgate Thirty Club.

(NINTH SEASON.)

Myself when young did eagerly frequent
Doctor and Saint, and heard great argument
About it and about : but evermore
Came out by the same door as in I went
—OMAR KHAYYAM.

❧ ❧ ❧ ❧

THE

# Annual Dinner

TO BE HELD AT

"THE OLD CROWN"

ASSEMBLY HALL

## On Saturday, May 6th, 1911,

AT 6.30 P.M. SHARP.

❧ ❧ ❧ ❧

*Chairman :*
H. VAN HOOYDONK.

*Musical Director :*
W. GRIFFITHS.

## Officers of the Club.

———

*President.*
H. VAN HOOYDONK.

*Vice-President.*
W. K. JEALOUS.

*Hon. Treasurer.*
W. GRIFFITHS.

*Committee.*
W. B. PARTRIDGE.
J. A. BOLSTER.
B. D. GRAY.
CYRIL RENTON.
G. J. SYMONDS.
T. WOOLRIDGE.

*Hon. Sec. :* E. H. HILL,
34, Cromwell Avenue,
Highgate, N.

———

Woolridge & Co., Highgate.

Lauderdale House, Waterlow Park, seen here in about 1905, is a merchant's house built in 1582 for Sir Richard Martin, twice Lord Mayor of London. The house passed through several different owners until about 1642, when it was left to Lady Anne Lauderdale. It is rumoured that Lady Lauderdale let the house for a period to Charles II's mistress, Nell Gwynn, who lived there for a short time with her infant son, the Duke of St Albans. The house continued to change hands many times over the next 150 years and, towards the end of the eighteenth century, it became one of the many private boarding schools in Highgate. It reverted to a private house again in the early nineteenth century, when it was completely altered both inside and out. Lauderdale's last private owner was industrialist Sir Sidney Waterlow, who leased it for a time to St Bartholomew's Hospital as a convalescent home, but by 1883 the house lay empty. In 1889, Sir Sidney gave the house and grounds to the London County Council 'for the enjoyment of Londoners, a garden for the gardenless', after which the 29 acres of land became a public park. The house was restored in 1893 to serve for seventy years as a tearoom and park-keepers' flats. During the course of further renovation in 1963, a fire broke out, destroying the roof and much of the interior of the house. After fifteen years of lying derelict, the house was finally repaired and reopened in 1978 as a community cultural and educational centre, which is today operated by the Lauderdale House Society, a registered charity. Despite the fire, the house is one of the few in London that retains almost the entire original Tudor timber frame.

*Opposite, bottom left:* The Highgate Thirty Club programme and menu for their ninth annual dinner, held at the Old Crown Assembly Hall on Saturday, 6 May 1911. The Highgate Thirty Club was a social and debating group that was founded in 1902 and met each week at the Flask in the village. In 1906, the Highgate Thirty Club revived Highgate's ancient tradition of 'Swearing on the Horns', which had died out a few years earlier (*see* page 57).

*Opposite, bottom right:* In 1911, at the time of this dinner, Hubert Van Hooydonk, a Dutch designer and decorative painter, was president of the club. He lived at no. 9 Holly Terrace until his death in 1940. Walter K. Jealous was vice-president of the club; he later became editor of the *Hampstead and Highgate Express*, of which his late uncle, George Samuel Jealous, was the first known proprietor. In 1929, Walter became president of the Highgate Thirty Club. He lived at no. 7 Holly Terrace until his death in 1932.

Lauderdale House, Waterlow Park, Highgate, *c.* 1910. The grounds of Lauderdale House now make up Waterlow Park.

Waterlow Park and Lake with the domes of St Joseph's in the background, *c.* 1907. The park is adjacent to St Joseph's Church and covers 29 acres of beautiful sloping parkland with panoramic views across London.

People out walking in Waterlow Park, *c.* 1906. Sir Sidney Waterlow, former Lord Mayor of London, gave the park to the public in 1889, as 'a garden for the gardenless'. The park includes the historic Lauderdale House and its formal terraced gardens.

Waterlow Park and St Joseph's Church and Retreat, *c.* 1904. Today, the park boasts ponds on three levels, tree-lined walkways, mature shrub beds and herbaceous borders, ornamental bedding, rose gardens, expanses of lawn, six tennis courts, a putting green and a small dog-free play area for the under fives. The park is home to a variety of wildlife, including foxes and bats. It also has an aviary that is used as an injured animal recovery centre.

WATERLOW PARK, THE BAND STAND.

The Band Stand in Waterlow Park, *c.* 1904. In recent years, considerable restoration work has been carried out on this Grade II listed park and its buildings, including a new stone plinth for Sir Sydney Waterlow's statue. The statue features Sir Sydney holding the key to the park in one hand and his umbrella and hat in the other. In the summer, open-air concerts fill the grounds with music.

WINCHESTER HALL, HIGHGATE.
DEMOLISHED 1881.

W.W.WEST.

Winchester Hall, at the corner of Hornsey Lane and Highgate Hill, demolished in about 1881, from a drawing by W. West. The Winchester Hall Estate is said to be named after Susannah Winch who owned property there in the eighteenth century, called Winches House. The estate stretched from the west end of Hornsey Lane across to the north-east as far as Archway Road. When the then owner of Winchester Hall, Col J.W. Jeakes, died in 1874, his son sold it to the Imperial Property Investment Co. It was pulled down in about 1881 to make way for new housing to accommodate people moving into the area, encouraged by the opening of Highgate Station in 1867. Its fittings, including 1½ miles of iron park fencing, were sold. The demolition of Winchester Hall allowed for the widening of Hornsey Lane and the construction of Cromwell Avenue, Cromwell Place and Winchester Road through the estate.

Channing School, The Bank, Highgate Hill viewed from the north looking down Highgate Hill, c. 1905. Apart from the traffic, the scene has changed very little in the last 100 years. This independent school for girls is still situated in the same position that it occupied when it first opened at Sutherland House in 1885. Sisters Matilda and Emily Sharpe and the Revd Robert Spears, all members of the Unitarian Church, founded the school in 1885, primarily for the daughters of Unitarian ministers. The school was named after Dr William Ellery Channing, one of the leading Unitarian preachers in America in the early nineteenth century.

Miss Emily Sharpe and Miss Matilda Sharpe, c. 1910. The Sharpe sisters were keen for the girls to be taught a very wide range of subjects, which included many of their own favourites, such as: music, drama, history, literature, science, and Latin. The school uniform was compulsory, and the girls were encouraged to attend the Unitarian Church on Highgate Hill.

Channing School photograph, *c.* 1885. The number of girl pupils rose to about ninety in the first year and the numbers continued to rise at such a rate that in the 1920s, the school expanded into the neighbouring houses in the terrace.

Channing House School
The Bank
Highgate.
July 30th 1892.

Mrs Stephenson
to
Miss M. Sharpe
2nd term 1892.
School Fees for ½ term
£1 . 6 . 3.
received with
Thanks
Matilda Sharpe
Aug 3 1892.

Remittance advice from Mrs Stephenson for £1 6s 3d in school fees for the second term of 1892. It is signed as received by Matilda Sharpe, one of the founders and joint headmistresses of the school, *c.* 1892.

This picture of The Bank, looking down Highgate Hill, shows Sutherland House, the original school building of Channing House School, on the left at the junction of Highgate Hill and Cholmeley Park, *c.* 1904. The entrance to Waterlow Park is on the right.

The Andrew Marvell memorial plaque marks the site of Marvell's Cottage at the top of Highgate Hill. The plaque was mounted on the wall of Waterlow Park by the London County Council in December 1898 (photograph *c.* 2008).

ANDREW MARVEL'S HOUSE
HIGHGATE.
DEMOLISHED 1868.

Drawing by W. West of Andrew Marvell's Cottage, Highgate Hill, demolished in 1868. Andrew Marvell (1621–1678), English poet, wit, satirist and politician, lived in Highgate for a period during the 1670s. Marvell is now considered one of the greatest poets of the seventeenth century. He was born on 31 March 1621, in Winestead, near Kingston-upon-Hull, Yorkshire. He was educated at Hull Grammar School, and at the tender age of twelve he went to Trinity College, Cambridge, where he received his BA degree when he was eighteen. His first published poems were written in Latin and Greek while he was still at Cambridge. After leaving university, he travelled Europe, visiting France, Holland, Italy and Spain. He returned to England in 1646, having learned four languages during his travels. He then became a tutor for a few years, and from 1650 to 1652 he was tutor to Lord Fairfax's daughter, Mary, in Yorkshire. In 1653, he became tutor to Cromwell's ward, William Dutton, based at the house of John Oxenbridge, a fellow of Eton College. In 1657, Marvell was appointed assistant to his friend, poet John Milton, Latin Secretary to the Commonwealth. In 1659, Marvell was elected MP for his hometown of Hull, which he represented for the last twenty years of his life. He died suddenly on 16 August 1678, his death suspected to have been the result of an overdose of opiate taken during an attack of ague (a fever). He was buried in the church of St Giles-in-the-Fields, London. Andrew Marvell's time in Highgate is one of the area's great mysteries. According to Marvell's letters, he lived in the cottage at the top of Highgate Hill in the year 1675, at least. The cottage had access to what is now Waterlow Park, and it is thought that those parklands were the inspiration for Marvell's poem *The Garden*. The cottage was in use until 1866 and was finally demolished in 1868.

Cromwell House, Hospital for Sick Children, No. 104 Highgate Hill, *c*. 1905. Sir Richard Sprignell built Cromwell House in about 1630. It was rumoured that Oliver Cromwell had the house built for his son-in-law General Henry Ireton, but there is no evidence that either Cromwell or Ireton ever lived there. The Sprignell family owned the house until about 1664. Thereafter, the house had a succession of private owners until about 1833 when it became a boys' boarding school. In 1869, Cromwell House became the 'Country Branch' of Great Ormond Street Hospital.

Cromwell House, Hospital for Sick Children, rear view, *c*. 1905. In the late 1860s, the governors of Great Ormond Street Hospital decided to open a convalescent home near enough to the hospital to make visiting and transporting the children feasible, but away from the foul coal-filled air of central London. By 1885, Cromwell House provided care for ninety-eight convalescent and 152 chronic patients at any one time. There were large grounds to act as a playground and the children were encouraged to spend as much time out of doors as possible.

Cromwell House, Highgate, N.

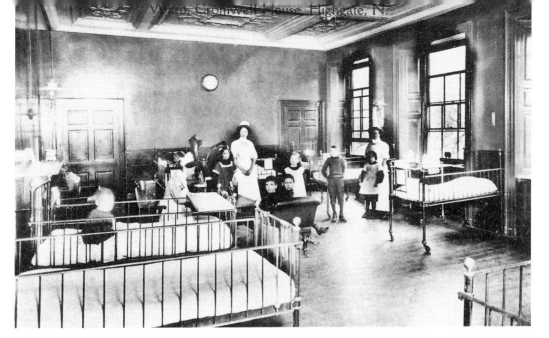

Cromwell House, Hospital for Sick Children ward, *c.* 1905. The nurses worked a twelve-hour day, beginning at 7.30 a.m., with each nurse looking after between nine and twelve children. In those days, in addition to their medical duties, the nurses looked after the hard labour of the house. During their working day they would wash and dress their children, dress the wounds, take temperatures, administer medicines, make the beds, serve the meals and attend to their patients' comfort. They also did the ward housework, washed bandages, rinsed soiled linen, and every third week they would do the crockery washing-up for a week. The nurses were allowed ten minutes for their lunch break, and twenty minutes for their dinner.

View of The Bank, Highgate Hill, with Cromwell House fronted with trees, *c.* 1907. Great Ormond Street Hospital kept Cromwell House open until the early 1920s, when it became clear that the old mansion was no longer suitable. They moved to a new convalescent home with parkland, near Epsom in Surrey. Today, the Ghana High Commission occupies Cromwell House. The building's façade has changed very little in the last 100 years.

Cromwell House, Highgate.

Furnival House, Cholmeley Park, Highgate, *c.* 1916. The house was designed by J.H. Pott and built in 1916 for the Prudential Assurance Co. to accommodate female staff from their head office in Holborn. From about 1928, the Whittington Hospital used it as a home for nurses. The building now belongs to the University of Westminster and is one of its seven halls of residence for students.

Santa Claus Home, Cholmeley Park, *c.* 1905. In 1885, the Santa Claus Society began sending toys at Christmas to children in hospital, the gifts being distributed by members. After a few years, the members thought it 'a pity that Santa Claus should sleep all summer', and in 1891 three sisters founded a Santa Claus Home of their own, for the benefit of children suffering from spinal and hip diseases. The first home was in their private house at no. 34 South Grove (later no. 69 Highgate West Hill). In 1889, Baroness Angela Burdett-Coutts became patroness of the Society. In 1900, The Santa Claus Home for Sick Children moved to no. 55 Cholmeley Park, and two of the sisters, Miss Henrietta F. Charles and Miss Janie F. Charles, continued to manage the home for many years after. The home was closed around 1954 when the London County Council acquired it for tuberculosis patients.

# 3

# The Village

Highgate, South Grove, *c.* 1920. The High Street and its surroundings managed to keep its country village feel well into the nineteenth century. Being only 6 miles from the city centre, its clean air and panoramic views continually attracted Londoners looking for a healthy retreat from the pressures of city life and the city smog. Although it was mainly the wealthy that bought houses in the area, the advent of trams, buses and train services from central London to Highgate gave ordinary Londoners the opportunity to spend their days off in the parks and woods on the hill. Even today, despite twenty-first century road traffic pollution and the expanding population, it still retains its unique village atmosphere. Many eighteenth and nineteenth-century brick-built shops and houses can still be seen around the village, including several English Heritage listed buildings.

Fairseat House, High Street, as viewed from the rear garden, is set in extensive gardens with spectacular views across London, *c.* 1980. In the nineteenth century, Fairseat was the family home of Sir Sydney Waterlow, former Lord Mayor of London, a wealthy wholesale stationer and printer. He named the mansion after that of his late father-in-law, Mr William Hickson, of Fairseat, Wrotham, Kent. Sir Sydney rebuilt the house in 1867. The east-wing was demolished in 1909 to allow for widening the top of Highgate Hill to make space for a double track to be laid for the new electric tramway. Fairseat is situated at the top of Highgate Hill at no. 1 High Street, on the site of the house in which Sir Roger Cholmeley lived in the sixteenth century. Since 1926, Fairseat has been the home of Channing Junior School, founded in 1885.

*Opposite:* High Street, Highgate, *c.* 1904. The view, facing south, is of an Edwardian lady getting on a cable tramcar outside Attkins, the pork butchers, in the High Street. The tram hides the Prince of Wales public house from view. The cable tramway operated, off and on, between 1884 and 1909 but was out of use from 1892 to 1897. It fell into disrepair in 1906–7, having suffered with competition from the electric trams that started service along Archway Road in 1905. The Highgate Hill cable tramway was closed in 1909 and reopened as an electric tramway in 1910.

The Old Forge
High St Highgate - 1882

*Above:* Highgate High Street as it was in 1882, showing the old forge. This was known as Dodd's Corner, after the name of the blacksmith. A smithy on this site can be traced back as far 1664. The old forge was demolished in *c.* 1896.

HIGHGATE. --- A Cable Tramcar.

93.

45

High Street, Highgate Village, *c.* 1905. This view is looking downhill to the south, with a cable-drawn tram approaching and terminating at Highgate Village. The Angel Inn is on the right of the picture.

High Street, Highgate, facing north with the old Gate House Tavern in the distance, *c.* 1906. The Prince of Wales public house and the Highgate Cycle Works are on the left. Randall's butcher's shop is on the right, and just beyond that is the Rose and Crown public house.

*Highgate Village*

A sketch of High Street by an unknown artist from the 1950s showing a view to the south, with the Angel Inn on the right.

Trolleybus terminal, Highgate Village, c. 1960. Trolleybuses replaced tramcars in 1938, and buses replaced trolleybuses around 1961.

Prickett & Ellis at no. 4 Highgate High Street, with W.H. 'Tony' Ellis, nephew of Henry, on the right, *c.* 1953. The history of this business can be traced back to 1767 when carpenter John Prickett held a property auction in the village. In 1842, Frederick Prickett became the first Highgate historian, at the age of twenty-one, with the publication of his book, *The History and Antiquities of Highgate*. By 1892, the Prickett family had left the business but partner Henry Ellis continued as a sole trader. The first village office was at no. 32 High Street, moving to no. 4 in the 1930s and in the 1960s to no. 27 where it has remained to this day, now trading under the name of Prickett & Ellis, Underhill.

A drawing of Kent's Yard by W. West, *c.* 1905. Kent's Yard (now enclosed by gates) is next to no. 58 High Street. It was named after an early occupant, George Kent, a corn chandler.

Passengers alight from a cable tramcar near to the Prince of Wales pub in the High Street, *c.* 1905. Most of the cable track on Highgate Hill was double tracked except for about 1,000ft of track along the High Street that were single tracked. The cable-house was situated at the top of the hill on the east side of the High Street, near Townsend Yard.

Pond Square, Highgate, *c.* 1956. There used to be two ponds in Pond Square with a roadway separating them. For centuries, these two ponds had been used as a source of water for the poor. In about 1844, one was filled in and the other, which spread across part of what is now South Grove, was made smaller. The roadway that previously divided the two ponds was then abolished and South Grove was widened. In around 1864, the remaining pond was filled in because it had become an eyesore and was considered to be a danger to public health. Pond Square is one of the most ancient parts of Highgate and has changed very little over the last century.

Church House, no. 10 South Grove, *c*. 2008. Church House was built in the early eighteenth century and owned by Sir John Hawkins (Samuel Johnson's biographer) and his wife, Sidney from 1759–1782. In 1799, it became a ladies' boarding school, and from 1802–1843, a Jewish boys' school. Church House is said to have been the model for the 'old brick house at Highgate on the very summit of the hill' where the Steerforths lived in Charles Dickens' novel, *David Copperfield*, *c*. 1850. Henry Beck (also known as Harry Beck), best known for his 1933 geometric design of the London Transport Underground map that is still in use today, lived at Church House in the 1920s.

The Highgate Literary & Scientific Institution (est. 1839), no. 11 South Grove, and the Highgate Society (est. 1966), no. 10a South Grove, c. 2008. The Highgate Literary & Scientific Institution was founded by a group of Highgate residents in 1839. Their first home was in the then Southwood Terrace in Southwood Lane. In 1840, they rented some outbuildings in South Grove from Leopold Neumegen who ran the Jewish Boys' School next door at Church House. The Institution had the first library in the village and they held lectures in a converted stable block. The Institution provided an alternative social meeting place for the well-off residents (early membership was one guinea), who were previously limited to entertaining at home or mixing with the local riff-raff in public-houses. The present-day building dates back to about 1880, when the Institution redeveloped it. The Institution still thrives today as one of only a handful of such independent institutions remaining. In addition to its ever-growing library, it now provides members with a varied programme of cultural activities.

Next door, no. 10a South Grove (built 1848) is home to the Highgate Society. Formed in 1966, this is a voluntary organisation of over 1,000 members living in and around Highgate. Their primary aims are to make Highgate a better place in which to live and work. The Society is the modern-day equivalent of the earlier Highgate Preservation Society, which was formed in 1935 and campaigned to protect Highgate buildings. In the late 1930s, they unsuccessfully opposed the use of trolleybuses in the village.

Moreton House, no. 14 South Grove, Highgate, c. 2008. Built in 1715 for Roger Young and restored in 1978, its upper floors were again rebuilt and refurbished in 1983 following serious fire damage. The house is best known for its most famous resident, Samuel Taylor Coleridge (1772–1834), the poet, critic and philosopher. Apart from his poetic talents, Coleridge was renowned for his addiction to opium, and in the latter part of his life, he was said to be using as much as two quarts of laudanum a week. He was born in Ottery St Mary, Devon, the son of a vicar and the youngest of ten children. As a child, he would take refuge in the local library to escape some of the bullying by one of his elder brothers, and it was there that he discovered his passion for poetry. He attended Christ's Hospital Boarding Grammar School in London, and went on to study at Jesus College, Cambridge. In his early twenties, he met and became friends with the poet William Wordsworth. As a young man, Coleridge suffered a lot with toothaches and, at the age of twenty-five, he started taking opium to help with the pain. At the time he had no idea that this would damage his health and lead him to become addicted to the drug. Coleridge moved around quite a bit in his life, living in Devon, London, Somerset, Germany, Keswick in the English Lake District, Malta and Sicily. By 1817, his addiction to opium had worsened to the extent that he sought the help of London physician James Gillman. Later that year he moved into the Gillman family home at Moreton House in South Grove, Highgate, and he moved with them to no. 3 The Grove in 1823. For seventeen years Dr Gillman and his family managed to keep Coleridge's addiction under control until he finally died in 1834 as a result of heart and lung complications caused by his opium addition. He was buried in the aisle of St Michael's Church, Highgate.

Samuel Taylor Coleridge, c. 1814.

St Michael's Church, South Grove, *c.* 1906. The church was built in 1832 by William and Thomas Cubitt from the designs of Lewis Vulliamy (1791–1871). It is London's highest church and stands on the site of Ashurst House, an old manor house built around 1690 for Sir William Ashurst (1647–1719), who was Lord Mayor of London *c.*1693. The foundations of the demolished Ashurst House are beneath the church. It was originally in the parish of St Pancras, but St Michael's soon became the parish church of Highgate Village. The church was restored in about 1950 following war damage. Samuel Taylor Coleridge is buried in the aisle of St Michael's Church, just a short distance from his home in The Grove. He was originally buried at Old Highgate Chapel but was re-interred in St Michael's Church in 1961. The church featured in Sir John Betjeman's (1906–1984), Highgate inspired, autobiographical book of verse, *Summoned by Bells* (*c.* 1960). To the left of the picture is the eighteenth-century Flask Inn, and behind that, next to St Michael's, is the splendid red-brick Old Hall (rebuilt around 1694), which is the largest residence in South Grove.

Highgate Cemetery (East), Swains Lane, Highgate, *c.* 2008. Highgate Cemetery, a Grade II listed park, is in fact a combination of two cemeteries that are situated in Swains Lane and cover some 37 acres of sloping land on the former grounds of the Ashurst Estate. The original Western Cemetery was opened in 1839 and it soon became the most sought after and fashionable cemetery in London. Its popularity resulted in it being extended to the other side of the road in 1854 (the Eastern Cemetery). English Heritage lists Highgate Cemetery as place of 'outstanding historical and architectural interest'. This is thanks to a group of local supporters who formed the Friends of Highgate Cemetery (FOHC) in October 1975 to help save the cemetery from ruin. The FOHC, a registered charity, acquired the freehold to both parts of the cemetery in 1981, and it is now entirely managed by them. Over the years, the cemetery has been restored and developed by FOHC, with the help and financial support of the Manpower Services Commission, English Heritage, FOHC subscribing members and on-site volunteers. Today, the original Western Cemetery is closed, but guided tours are conducted by FOHC at specific times on most days. The Eastern Cemetery is open to the public daily.

Highgate Cemetery and St Michael's Church, *c.* 1905. This view is from the summit of the old Western Cemetery, with the Beer family's mausoleum to the left and St Michael's Church standing high above the terrace. Highgate Cemetery is best known as the place where Karl Marx (1818–1883) is buried, and his grave is still a popular stop off for tourists. However, the plot where he now lies under a huge granite bust in the Eastern Cemetery was not his original resting place. In 1954, he was moved from the other side of the cemetery after a group of communist sympathisers funded the purchase of a new burial plot and the erection of a grand bust of Marx with the inscription, 'Workers of the World Unite', to replace his original simple headstone.

There are at least another 850 notable names among the 51,000 or so headstones. These include such well-known names as Michael Faraday, Mary Ann Evans (alias George Eliot) and Sir Ralph Richardson. There are six Lord Mayors of London and many founders of London businesses, including John Maple of the Tottenham Court Road furniture store, William Alfred Foyle of the Charing Cross Road bookshop and John Lobb of the world famous St James Street boot shop. Other notable and diverse characters include Baron Dalziel, who introduced motor cabs to London in 1907, Charles Chubb of Chubb Lock fame, Charles Cruft, founder of the supreme dog show, cinematography pioneer William Friese-Green and the popular comic, Max Wall.

The Flask Inn, South Grove, with St Michael's Church spire in the background, *c.* 1905. Now addressed as 77 Highgate West Hill, the Flask dates back to the early eighteenth century. It is one of the few Highgate pubs where the annual custom of 'Swearing on the Horns' still takes place. This old ceremony is thought to have originated when drovers stopped off in Highgate on their way to the London cattle markets. It involved swearing an oath over some animal horns, which later evolved into a swearing-in ceremony for Freeman of Highgate.

The Flask Inn, South Grove, *c.* 1905. The famous Highgate Flask is said to get its name from the tradition of visitors to the local Hampstead springs stopping off at the pub to buy a flask to transport the waters home. Legend has it that the highwayman Dick Turpin (1705–1739) avoided capture by hiding in the pub's cellars. The eighteenth-century painter and satirist William Hogarth (1697–1764) is said to have been a regular at the Flask.

Old Gate House, from a photograph of the late nineteenth century, several years before its renovation in 1905. The Gatehouse pub is also home to London's top theatre, being 446ft above sea level, and it is probably the oldest known inn in Highgate. The earliest mention of the Gatehouse in licensing records is 1670, but it has been claimed by previous owners that there has been an inn on the site since 1337. There was certainly a licensed premise on the site before 1670, but earlier licensing records only made mention of the number of licensed premises in Highgate, not their names. The Gatehouse got its name from the original fourteenth-century building that was connected to the gate (the tollgate being removed in 1892) that crossed the road here. It is said to be where the Highgate custom of 'Swearing on the Horns' originated in the seventeenth century. It was a sort of fraternity started by drovers that stayed overnight in Highgate on their way to the London cattle markets. In its simplest form, the 'Swearing on the Horns' ceremony consisted of newcomers taking an oath confirming their dedication to merriment and debauchery. It involved kissing or saluting a set of animal horns and agreeing to a number of statements that were usually read out by the pub's landlord wearing some formal robes. The immediate reward, after swearing on the horns, was that the participant could kiss the prettiest woman in the pub. It was one of the earliest known tourist traps. In the eighteenth century, throughout the country, it was quite usual to ask, 'Have you been sworn at Highgate?' George Cruikshank, Lord Byron and Charles Dickens were all said to have been regulars here during the early nineteenth century.

SIR R. CHOLMELEY'S SCHOOLS, HIGHGATE, LATELY REBUILT.

*Opposite, top:* Ye Old Gate House, Highgate around 1905, just after its renovation in the mock-Tudor style in which it remains today. Next to the hotel and lounge entrance is a board advertising its 'Highgate Hall, a place suitable for Balls, Cinderellas, Concerts, Wedding Receptions and Meetings'. It was famous all over London for its 'shilling ordinaries', which were enormous lunches.

*Opposite, centre:* Highgate School, North Road, *c.* 1904. Although the school is still referred to as Sir Roger Cholmeley's School, it has been called Highgate School since the latter part of the nineteenth century. Highgate School is one of the best-known independent schools in the country and has educated many famous people throughout its long history.

*Opposite, bottom:* Highgate School and Chapel (Sir Roger Cholmeley's School), North Road, from an original engraving, *c.* 1867. Sir Roger Cholmeley (1485–1565), former Lord Chief Justice of England and landowner, lived in a house on the site of where Fairseat now stands in the High Street. He established Highgate School by Royal Charter of Her Majesty Queen Elizabeth I, just before his death in 1565. It began as a free school for the education of boys and young men in grammar. The school was small and so a total of just forty free scholars were drawn from Highgate and the surrounding villages. The school also had a chapel which provided the spiritual needs of the boys and villagers. The original schoolhouse and chapel were modified and rebuilt several times but the number of pupils did not increase until about 1839 when John Bradley Dyne became headmaster and set out to increase the number of fee-paying pupils. By 1865, the school had forty free scholars and ninety fee-paying pupils, and the school was becoming increasingly popular with local well-to-do families. The present main school in North Road was built in 1866 and the new chapel consecrated the following year. The school continued to expand its facilities over the next few years through property and land acquisitions in Southwood Lane, Broadlands Road, Bishopswood Road and Hampstead Lane. In 1889, the Highgate Junior School was established by the then headmaster, the Revd Charles McDowell.

By the end of the nineteenth century, the teaching of science and technical skills was on the increase, and in 1897 these were moved to a separate science building. By now, Highgate School was being recognised as a leading English public school, competing with Eton, Harrow and Winchester. The need for science and technical knowledge continued to grow and, in 1928, a new science block was built. It was designed to contain not only science and biology laboratories but also facilities for the study of engineering and aeronautics. There was also a new library and a large lecture room. In 1938, the Junior School was moved to the then newly purpose-built Cholmeley House in Bishopswood Road.

Most of the main school buildings were taken over by the British government when the Second World War began in 1939. Teaching went on in those buildings that remained, but most of the staff and pupils were evacuated to Westward Ho! (Devon). The boys lived and were taught in hotels and boarding houses which had been taken over for this purpose. In 1943, the school was obliged for financial reasons to return to London and its buildings in Highgate were handed back to them. By the 1960s the school's property and land occupied large areas of Highgate Village. In more recent years, the buildings have been further extended and modernised to increase its combined number of pupils to over 1,200. The school has recently started moving towards becoming fully co-educational, thus ending over 400 years of single-sex education.

Many old boys, called Old Cholmeleians after the school's founder Sir Roger Cholmeley, went on to achieve great success in a wide variety of professions. Old Cholmeleians include: Sir John Betjeman, Poet Laureate and author; John Leyton, actor and singer; Michael Mansfield, QC; Barry Norman, film critic and author; Geoffrey Palmer, actor; Robin Ray, broadcaster; Sir Clive Sinclair, inventor; Philip Tufnell, England and Middlesex cricketer; Murray Walker, motor racing commentator.

Highgate School Hall in about the 1950s.

# 4

# *West Hill Area*

Highgate West Hill, *c.* 1910. This view approaches the top of West Hill with no. 39 on the left and just beyond, the site of the old Fox and Crown Inn (demolished 1896) where now stands the recently renovated Summit House, renamed the Summit (no. 40) and currently being used as a private health centre. The large wall on the left stretching from no. 40 to the top of West Hill hides and secures the seventeenth-century Parkfield Estate, part of which became the Witanhurst Estate when Sir Arthur Crosfield built Witanhurst in about 1913–20.

Witanhurst Gatehouse built in about the 1920s, at the top of Highgate West Hill, c. 2008. This is the main entrance to the Witanhurst Estate, which occupies a large part of the 11½ acre ancient Parkfield Estate. The main Witanhurst house, a Grade II listed building, is set back beyond these gates. It is London's second largest private house, dwarfed only by Buckingham Palace. In recent years, apart from occasional use as a film setting for television, it has been empty. Set within 5½ acres, with three separate gatehouses, it was designed for wealthy soap magnate, Sir Arthur Crosfield. It took seven years to build and work was finally completed in 1920. The house has sixty-five rooms, including a 70ft ballroom. Witanhurst was sold to a property developer in June 2007 for £32 million, and it is reportedly now up for sale again with a price tag of £75 million.

*Opposite, bottom:* Lissenden Mansions, Lissenden Gardens, c. 1906. This is a view that John Betjeman would have looked out upon from his birth home in Parliament Hill Mansions before his family moved half a mile up the road to no. 31 Highgate West Hill in c. 1908. John Betjeman's family had moved to England more than a century earlier and settled in Islington where they built up a furniture manufacturing business. Their name 'Betjemann' was changed to the less Germanic 'Betjeman' during the First World War. The young John Betjeman went to Highgate School and was taught by the famous poet, dramatist and literary critic, T.S. Eliot. Betjeman was very attached to the area he grew up in and referred to it in many of his poems, in particular in his autobiographical book of verse, *Summoned by Bells* (1960). As well as being a successful broadcaster, Betjeman became a popular television performer, which brought his poetry to an enormous audience. He was awarded the CBE in 1960 and became Poet Laureate in 1972. During the latter part of his life Betjeman suffered from Parkinson's disease. He died at his home in Cornwall on 19 May 1984 at the age of seventy-seven.

*Above:* Highgate West Hill, showing the white milestone on the right of the picture outside the entrance to the Baroness Burdett-Coutts's estate, now Robin Grove, *c.* 1905. The Highgate-born Poet Laureate, writer and broadcaster, Sir John Betjeman, lived near here at no. 31 Highgate West Hill from about 1908 to 1917. The house now bears an English Heritage blue plaque to commemorate Betjeman's life and works.

The Fox and Crown Inn, Highgate West Hill, *c.* 1890. This inn, now demolished, was famous for the assistance given by the landlord, James Turner, to Queen Victoria when her carriage was involved in an accident while descending Highgate West Hill in 1837. Soon afterwards, Victoria rewarded the landlord with the Royal Coat of Arms, which can be seen above the door in the photograph and which is now in the library of the Highgate Literary & Scientific Institution.

The Summit, no. 40 Highgate West Hill, *c.* 2008. The Summit was built on the site of the Fox and Crown Inn which was demolished in about 1896. It has recently been refurbished and is now occupied by a private health clinic.

These two pages are from a leaflet produced in 1898 to promote the Cutbush Nurseries. In 1804, William Cutbush took over William Bowstread's existing garden nursery at the top of Highgate West Hill, on the site of the old White Hart Inn. In 1834, William Cutbush built his own house and shop on West Hill (now no. 80), which was to be Highgate's first garden centre. The nursery-gardening firm prospered and in 1855 William's son James took over from his father. In 1859, James convened a meeting that resulted in the formation of the Highgate Horticultural and Floricultural Society. In those early days, the Highgate Horticultural shows were held at Holly Lodge and Kenwood. The society still exists today and is one of the oldest horticultural societies in the UK. By 1871, the William Cutbush & Son nurseries were employing twenty-five men and two boys and had additional premises in Finchley. William's grandsons, William and Herbert, took over when James died in 1885 and, in 1897, they gained a Royal Warrant from the then Prince of Wales (later King Edward VII). William and Herbert continued to manage the business into the twentieth century, with branches in Highgate, Barnet and Bishopsgate in the City of London. They boasted the Highgate Nurseries to be 'the largest nurseries near London, where everything for the garden can be procured'. Early in the twentieth century, William Bignell, a former employee who then had his own rival business in North Road, took over the business. The property finally passed out of the Cutbush family's hands in 1915, by which time the nurseries held warrants from Queen Victoria and George V.

View of Highgate and Highgate Ponds from Parliament Hill, *c.* 1910. The prominent structure of St Joseph's Church and Retreat can be seen on the hill in the distance.

A swallow dive by Mr Mauritzi at Highgate Ponds, *c.* 1898. In 1893, the first diving stage in England was erected at the Highgate Pond. It was a firm board fixed at a height of about 15ft (4.6m) above the surface. In 1895, the Royal Life Saving Society staged the first National Graceful Diving Competition for men only at Highgate. A temporary structure was fitted each summer to allow competition divers to do running swallow-dives from heights of between 15ft (4.6m) and 33ft (10m). In about 1898, Messrs Johansson, Nagberg and Mauritzi came over from Sweden and demonstrated the art of fancy high diving from a 10m platform erected at Highgate Pond. This resulted in the formation of the Amateur Diving Association in 1901, the first official organisation in the world devoted to the sport of diving. The Highgate Diving Club, founded in 1928 and based at Highgate Ponds, was the first British diving club. By 1939 the club was attracting crowds of up to 10,000 spectators to their diving exhibitions at Highgate and they dominated the British diving competitions.

Women Bathers at Highgate Ponds, *c.* 1908. London County Council had ruled in 1902 that the bathing pond at Parliament Hill was reserved for women throughout the whole of Wednesday all year round. The only condition imposed upon the bathers was that the Amateur Swimming Association must approve the costumes they wore.

Parliament Hill Cricket Ground on the Heath near to Highgate Road, *c.* 1907. This area of the Heath, to the south of Parliament Hill, is still dedicated to sport today, with cricket and football pitches, tennis courts, a bowling green, an athletics track and of course, the lido.

*Opposite*: Angela Georgina Burdett-Coutts was born in London on 21 April 1814, the youngest daughter of Sir Francis Burdett. She took the name Coutts in 1837 when she inherited the Coutts' family banking fortune from her grandfather, the banker, Sir Thomas Coutts, making her, after Queen Victoria, the wealthiest woman in England. Angela was a natural philanthropist but she was greatly influenced by two of her best friends, Charles Dickens and the Duke of Wellington, when choosing which charities to support and how to protect her wealth from con-artists and gold-diggers. Her inheritance included the Holly Lodge Estate on Highgate West Hill, which soon became her country house where she held large extravagant parties.

She was a clever businesswoman and took a keen interest in the running of Coutts Bank. However, her main interest was in the welfare of others and during the course of her life, she spent most of her inherited wealth on a wide range of philanthropic causes. Her caring disposition did not prevent her from taking some extreme actions to keep people of a lower social class from encroaching on the luxury and privacy of her Holly Lodge Estate. In 1856, she bought nos. 78–79 Highgate West Hill, and a year later she bought South Grove House in order to prevent the purchase of these by undesirable neighbours. In 1861, she attempted to close a long-established public footpath that ran across her land from the bottom of Swains Lane to an exit at South Grove House, on the grounds that courting couples were using it. She was compassionate to the poor but believed that they should keep their lowly place in society and remain subservient. For a woman of such intelligence and achievement, she was surprisingly suspicious of education for women unless it was of a domestic nature. When she set up her house of rescue for prostitutes, or 'fallen women', as she called them, on the recommendation and guidance of Dickens, who helped to set up the home, she insisted that the women should wear a plain, modest uniform, be guided in religion and be taught the humble skills of sewing, cooking and knitting, with a view to them eventually gaining some related future employment.

The poor of London's East End were beneficiaries of several Burdett-Coutts's charity projects, and to them she became known as the 'Queen of the Poor'. In 1871, she was the first woman to be created a baroness in her own right. In 1872, she was the first woman to receive the Freedom of the City of London, and, in 1874, she was made Edinburgh's first woman Burgess and given the Freedom of the City of Edinburgh. In 1881, at the age of sixty-seven, she shocked polite society when she married her secretary, an American man who was only thirty. Unusually, Angela's husband changed his name to Mr Burdett-Coutts, but he did not become a baron.

Angela Georgina Burdett-Coutts died of acute bronchitis on 30 December 1906, at no. 1 Stratton Street, Piccadilly, the house where she was born. Her funeral was held on 5 January 1907 at Westminster Abbey and was a very grand event that was attended by huge numbers of people from a whole range of society, including royalty. She is buried near the west door in the nave of Westminster Abbey. The London street names of Baroness Road, Burdett Road and Coutts Crescent help remind Londoners of her life-changing benevolence to London's poor.

Projects that Angela Burdett-Coutts financed or contributed to, included: Urania Cottage Home (for prostitutes) in Lime Grove, London; Church of St John in Limehouse, London; sewing school in Brown's Lane, Spitalfields; Columbia Market, Bethnal Green; Santa Claus Home for Disabled Children, Highgate (1890–1958); Ragged Schools Union, Burdett-Coutts's donations helped set up 350 schools for the purpose of teaching poor children without charging fees; the Temperance Society; National Society for the Prevention of Cruelty to Children; National Society for the Prevention of Cruelty to Animals; Westminster Technical Institute; financial support to the people of south-west Ireland during the famine (1845–1852); fishermen of Baltimore, Co Cork, Ireland, to restore their fishing industry; the sponsoring of artists who were struggling to pay their rent; President British Beekeepers Association (1878–1906); President of the Ladies Committee of the RSPCA (England/Scotland); and lifeboats in Brittany, France.

She also funded many soup kitchens, working-class housing schemes, the building of some Anglican churches and even drinking fountains for dogs.

Electric trams (nos 755 and 937) in Highgate Road, with Grove Terrace running parallel on the right, *c.* 1911.

Holly Lodge, Highgate West Hill, from an original engraving, *c.* 1867. In July 1867, Miss Burdett-Coutts entertained more than 2,000 Belgian Rifle Volunteers, with about 500 other guests, in the pleasant grounds of her suburban villa, Holly Lodge, Highgate.

Holly Lodge Estate, seen here in about 1924, was sold in 1922 following the death of Baroness Burdett-Coutts' husband, William Lehman Ashmead Bartlett Burdett-Coutts (1851–1921). The house was demolished in 1923 by its new owner, Alderman Abraham Davis JP, who immediately had plans drawn up to build an estate of new houses for middle-class families and mansion block flats for single women who worked as secretaries and clerks in the City of London.

Holly Lodge Gardens in the 1930s. In 1926, the Central London Building Co. advertised the mock-Tudor styled estate as 'London's loveliest garden colony'. Its location and stunning views over London continue to make the Holly Lodge Estate of today a very popular place to live.

Langbourne Avenue, Holly Lodge Estate, *c.* 1946. The mock-Tudor style is very evident here with the towering Langbourne Mansions, the first mansion blocks to be built on the Holly Lodge Estate by the Lady Workers' Homes Limited in 1923. These provided eighty-eight self-contained flats for single women.

The restaurant at no. 30 Makepeace Avenue, Holly Lodge Estate, *c.* 1946. The Makepeace Avenue and Oakeshott Avenue mansion blocks were built as bedsits with no kitchens. This restaurant block was built as somewhere for the community to gather for meals. It included a restaurant, reading and meeting rooms and a small theatre. The block fell into disrepair during the late 1950s and was later demolished and replaced by a new community centre building.

Hillway, *c.* 1930. A notable resident of Hillway for many years was Andrew Rothstein (1898–1994), writer on communism and founder member of the British Communist Party. In 1956, he spoke at the occasion of the unveiling of Karl Marx's memorial bust in Highgate Cemetery.

Holly Lodge Gardens, *c.* 1960. Part of Holly Lodge Gardens is built on the site of the old Holly Lodge House (demolished 1923). One notable resident from about 1960 to 1973 was Denis Healey (born 1917), British Labour politician and Chancellor of the Exchequer from 1974–79.

Merton Lane, looking towards Millfield Lane and the ponds, *c.* 1903. John Henry Lloyd (1830–1910) lived at Greenbank (now demolished) in Merton Lane in the late nineteenth century. He was a Highgate historian and wine merchant, credited for saving the Highgate Literary & Scientific Institution from potential closure in the 1880s following years of decline. He initiated a fundraising and rebuilding program that helped the Instutute flourish into what it is today.

Millfield Lane, seen here in about 1906, bordering the eastern section of Hampstead Heath, is rumoured to have been the ancient route to the north linking Highgate Road with Hampstead Lane, before the upper Highgate West Hill existed. The famous nineteenth-century comedian Charles Mathews (1776–1835), a favourite of Charles Dickens, lived in Ivy Cottage (demolished) now the site of West Hill Court. One notable twentieth-century resident was Baroness Edith Summerskill (1901–1980), a physician, active feminist, Labour politician and writer, who lived at Pond House from 1951 until her death in 1980.

Highgate West Hill, with Millfield Lane on the right and St Anne's Church spire showing above the houses on the left, *c.* 1950. In the early days of motoring West Hill was a popular test hill for motorists.

15869 ST. ANN'S CHURCH HIGHGATE.

St Anne's Church, Highgate West Hill, seen here in about 1905, stands on the site of a seventeenth-century inn called the Cow and Hare, demolished during the late eighteenth century and replaced by a cottage bearing the same name. In 1837, the cottage was demolished and a house built on the site. In 1851, Anne Barnett, at her own expense, built the church of St Anne's (consecrated in 1853) in memory of her brother, Richard Barnett, who had recently died. She also donated her house for use as the vicarage. Baroness Angela Burdett-Coutts donated a peal of bells to the church. In about 1906, Sir John Betjeman was baptised at St Anne's and he referred to the church at least once in his poetry. This Anglican church is still in use today.

Dartmouth Park Hill, seen here in about 1928, was once part of Maiden Lane, a route through to Highgate that included York Way, Brecknock Road and Dartmouth Park Hill. Today, Maiden Lane is just a tiny side street off York Road.

1551S ST. PETERS CHURCH.                HIGHGATE.

St Peter's Church (built in about 1880), at the junction of Dartmouth Park Hill and Bredgar Road, *c.* 1906. The church has recently been converted into luxury apartments.

Kenwood House (south entrance), Hampstead Lane, *c*. 1930. Kenwood House, also known as the Iveagh Bequest, is in Hampstead Lane on the northern edge of Hampstead Heath. The original house was built here in the early seventeenth century and some remnants of it can be found in the basement area of the present building. In 1754, William Murray, 1st Earl of Mansfield, acquired Kenwood House and commissioned its rebuilding. He employed Robert Adams as the architect to create the beautiful structure we see today.

Kenwood House (north entrance), Hampstead Lane, *c*. 1930. In 1925, Edward Cecil Guinness, 1st Earl of Iveagh and Guinness brewery magnate, bought the house for £107,900. He bequeathed the estate to the benefit of the public when he died in 1927. It is now in the care of English Heritage.

Caen Wood Towers, Hampstead Lane, Highgate, from a woodblock print, *c.* 1880. Now called Athlone House, it stands on the site of Dufferin Lodge (demolished 1869), on ground that originally formed part of Fitzroy Park. Edward Brooke employed Messrs Salomons and Jones to design Caen Wood Towers in about 1870 and the building was completed in 1872. In its early years the grounds of Caen Wood Towers would sometimes be opened to the public for charitable garden parties. In both the First and Second World War, the house was used as a military convalescent hospital. The hospital, by now known as Athlone House Hospital, was made permanent after 1945. It later became a National Health Service facility, first used as a hospital and then as a nursing home. In about 2000, the facility became surplus to National Health Service requirements and the hospital was closed down permanently in September 2003. A private developer now owns the buildings.

The word *Caen*, in this context, is thought to be the ancient equivalent of the word *Ken*, hence the Kenwood Estate was once known as Caen Wood Estate.

# 5

# *North Hill Area*

Lower part of Southwood Lane, *c.* 1905. This timber-clad building, no. 80 Southwood Lane, displays an advertising board for F.L. Hall and Maple & Co. Decorator. By 1911, the building was occupied by W.F. Lowe, boot and shoemaker and A. Rowles, chimney-sweep and carpet beater.

Highgate Auxiliary Hospital, 'Byculla', Broadlands Road, Highgate, *c.* 1916. The building was used as a British Red Cross auxiliary hospital for wounded British soldiers by the War Office during the First World War, 1914–18. Recovering servicemen fill the windows and doorway to pose for the photograph. Smoking was a very popular habit with men during the First World War as it was said to calm their nerves. Most of the servicemen seen here are smoking cigarettes.

*Opposite, bottom:* Earlham School, Bishopswood Road, *c.* 1905. This private school for well-to-do young ladies was run by Miss Rigg and occupied one of the large detached houses (built around 1870s) on the edge of Highgate School playing fields from about the 1890s to 1920.

*Above:* Broadlands Road, *c.* 1904. The first buildings in Broadlands Road began to appear in 1878 when the Ecclesiastical Commissioners granted a lease to John Groom, architect, allowing him to build a development of large houses. These included Bishopsfield at no. 14 where John Sainsbury (1844–1928), founder of the Sainsbury's grocery stores (now supermarkets), lived *c.* 1899–1928. Groom also later worked on the two offshoots of Grange and Denewood Roads.

House of Mercy in about the 1920s, when it was a home for fallen women and unmarried mothers. In the mid-nineteenth century, it had been the Asylum for Idiots and was known as Park House. Demolished in 1946, it stood on the North Hill site where the Hillcrest development now stands.

In 1847, Revd Dr Andrew Reed completed a fact-finding mission in Europe where asylums for the feeble-minded had already been founded. He came back with a wealth of information, and, following public meetings that took place that year, it was resolved to found an institution for the remedial care and education of the feeble-minded. It was further resolved to proceed with the project 'The Asylum for Idiots' at Park House, and that 'it should be forthwith begun'. The asylum opened at Park House in 1848, with fifty-four boys and twelve girls admitted for training. It was the first institution of its kind in Britain, and its motto was 'Now There Is Hope'. Expansion was soon found necessary, and after a short temporary stay at Essex Hall, Colchester, the patients were moved in 1855 to the purpose-built Earlswood Asylum in Surrey.

Park House was later converted into the London Diocesan Penitentiary for prostitutes (fallen and penitent women) and renamed the House of Mercy. The laundry, with its large local clientele, provided most of the regular income for the House of Mercy. The penitentiary was taken over by nuns in 1900 and the penitents were alleged to have worked in silence. By the 1900s, the women were unmarried mothers rather than prostitutes as in Victorian times. In 1940, the establishment was closed and sold to Hornsey Council. After the Second World War the council pulled down the house and erected seven blocks of flats called Hillcrest.

NORTH HILL  Highgate

North Hill, *c.* 1906. The Bull pub (built *c.* 1765) at no. 13 North Hill underwent much rebuilding work in about 1906 but the frontage remained much the same in appearance and still does today. One notable North Hill resident was Charles Green (1785–1870), the most famous British balloonist of the nineteenth century. He lived at the then Aerial Cottage at no. 33 North Hill in the 1830s. By the time he retired in 1852, he had taken part in over 500 balloon flights, including in 1836 the then English long-distance ballooning record flight from London to Germany, 480 miles (772km), in eighteen hours.

North Road, *c.* 1905. The canopied shop to the right is that of Lake's Family Butcher's, and next to that is Appleton's Baker's, then Taylor's Grocer's, Bailey's Confectioner's, Smith's Greengrocer's, Webb's Corn Dealer's and Owen's Coffee Shop. All have since been demolished to make way for houses and the expansion of Highgate School.

Ye Olde Castle Coffee and Dining Rooms at no. 56 North Road on the corner of Castle Yard, around 1906, at the time owned by Fredrick Owen. This eighteenth-century building (now demolished) was home to the Castle Inn (licensed in 1719), which had a competition bowling green at the back and an attached converted barn that housed Highgate's only theatre in the early nineteenth century. The inn was closed in about 1872, but the building remained in use by the then Highgate Working Men's Club until it was converted into coffee rooms a few years later. It continued to be used as coffee and dining rooms until it was demolished in 1928.

Southwood Lane, Highgate

Southwood Lane, opposite the junction with The Park, *c*. 1905. On the left is the garden wall of Southwood House (eighteenth-century house demolished in the late 1950s), not to be confused with Southwood Hall in Muswell Hill Road. A policeman stands on the site of the old village well. On the right is the perimeter fence of Park House 'House of Mercy' (demolished 1946) and its grounds, which stretched across to North Hill where Hillcrest now stands.

Southwood Lane,
Highgate.

Southwood Lane, *c*. 1905. On the left are Sir Edward Pauncefort's twelve almshouses for poor widows and the two-storey schoolhouse for charity girls (all built in about 1722), rebuilt from the original Sir John Woolaston's six almshouses that were founded *c*.1658. Just a little way down on the right is Southwood Terrace (nos 24–48 built in about 1830) where the Highgate Literary & Scientific Institution had its first home at no. 24 (then no. 1 Southwood Terrace) in 1839.

Jackson's Lane, Highgate.

Southwood Lane with Jackson's Lane forking off to the right, *c.* 1905. In the middle is the whitewashed Bank Point Cottage, a late eighteenth-century house. At the time of this photograph, Southwood Lane separated the two old estates of Park House to the west, and Southwood House to the east. One notable resident of Southwood Lane was Mary Kingsley (1862–1900), English writer and explorer, who lived at no. 22 from 1863–1879 and spent most of that time at home caring for her invalid mother. Mary's travelling and exploring Africa didn't start until her mother and father both died in 1892.

# 6

# *Archway Road Area*

The Woodman, Archway Road at the junction of Muswell Hill Road, seen here in about 1905, was built in about 1828 to serve the increasing numbers of travellers along the Archway Road, which had opened just fifteen years earlier. This picture was taken shortly after the pub was rebuilt in 1905, with decorators' ladders still evident. The Woodman is now a locally listed building and therefore protected against insensitive development.

Archway Road was built in 1812–19 as a bypass (toll road) to the busy steep gradient of Highgate Hill and the narrow roads of Highgate Village. At the time, the new road ran through virtually open countryside. The area did not really start to develop until the opening of Highgate Railway Station in about 1867.

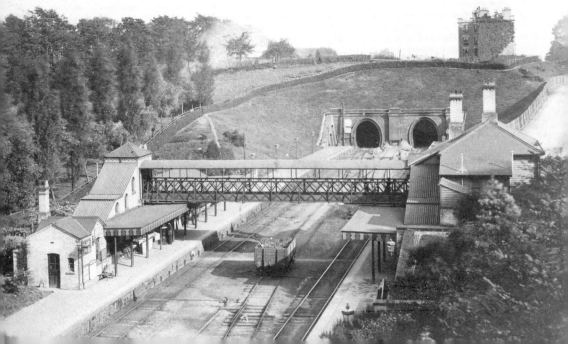

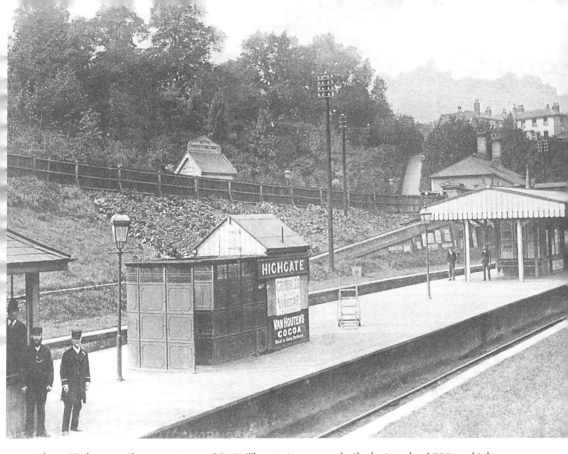

*Above:* Highgate railway station, *c.* 1900. The station was rebuilt during the 1880s, which included a new island platform with waiting shelter and a new booking office in the middle of the footbridge. In 1868, an additional entrance was provided on Archway Road, high above the station. The hut-like building beyond the wooden fence is an office of the Imperial Property Investment Co. Adverts on the side of the lavatory building include Grimble's Malt Vinegar, and Van Houten's Cocoa. British Railways (Eastern Region) closed the station to passengers on 5 July 1954 and closed the railway station completely on 1 October 1962, with the closure of its goods depot. The London Underground (tube station) Northern Line opened in 1941 with new deep-level platforms. The old surface platforms of the disused station are still there, but quite overgrown.

*Opposite, top:* Highgate railway station, *c.* 1885. The Great Northern Railway first opened the station on 28 August 1867. This view is facing west with the main station buildings on the left and the waiting shelter on the right. This picture shows the original side platforms with the main running tracks adjacent to each platform and a centre track that was used as a passing track for trains that terminated at Highgate. The covered footbridge ran from the upper floor of the main building to the brick-built stairwell on the other platform.

*Opposite, bottom:* Highgate station, *c.* 1885, looking east. The prominent four-storey building in the top right of the picture is Coleridge Buildings, built by the Highgate Dwelling Improvement Co. in 1867, demolished after being badly bomb damaged in the Second World War and replaced by Goldsmith's Court in 1950. To the right of that is the Birkbeck public house on the Archway Road, built some time around the 1860s, which became the Shepherds pub and is now called the Boogaloo.

THE MAIN AVENUE. HIGHGATE WOODS

Highgate Wood (previously known as Gravel Pit Wood), seen here in about 1910, was originally part of the Ancient Forest of Middlesex, and in the 1880s the then Bishop of London still privately owned it. Local people feared that the Ecclesiastical Commissioners might take advantage of its close proximity to Highgate station and build on the woodlands. A campaign was launched by Henry Reader Williams to save the wood, and in 1886 the City of London acquired it from the Ecclesiastical Commissioners for no charge but on condition that it was 'maintained in perpetuity for the benefit of Londoners'. Its name was then changed to Highgate Wood.

Highgate Wood, *c.* 1905. The opening of Highgate railway station in 1867 made Highgate Wood the ideal place for city dwellers to spend their Sundays to escape the streets of London and enjoy the country air and scenery.

Queen's Wood, seen here in about 1905, is an area of ancient woodland that originally formed part of the Middlesex Forest and was known as Churchyard Bottom Wood, possibly because of the discovery of human bones in the west of the wood, which were thought to be from a burial pit for victims of the Great Plague of 1665. In 1898, Churchyard Bottom Wood was purchased from the Ecclesiastical Commissioners by Hornsey Council, renamed Queen's Wood in honour of Queen Victoria, and opened to the public. It is now managed by the London Borough of Haringey. The pond in this photograph was replaced in 1935 by a concrete paddling pool.

Queen's Wood Pavilion, near Muswell Hill Road, seen here in about 1905, was originally built as a lodge for the head park keeper and his family. There was also a refreshment room that was used by visitors to the woods.

Southwood Hall, seen here in about 1906, was situated on the corner of Wood Lane and Muswell Hill Road. It was built in about 1845 for Henry Vertue Tebbs, a wealthy lawyer. It was a girls' school 'for daughters of gentlemen' from about 1905–1930. It was demolished in the early 1930s and replaced in 1937 with an up-market blocks of flats.

Southwood Hall School Dining Room, c. 1906. Southwood Hall should not be confused with Southwood House (demolished in late 1950s), which was in Southwood Lane.

Southwood Hall School and Garden, *c.* 1905. There were both boarders and day pupils at the school and the girls would help tend the large gardens. They had their own tennis courts and would play competitive tennis matches with girls from other local private schools, including Channing House School and North London Collegiate School.

*Below*: Schoolchildren pose for a photograph by the drinking fountain in Highgate Wood, *c.* 1908.

Wood Lane, *c.* 1910. In the early nineteenth century, Wood Lane was just a country track running from the Highgate end of Muswell Hill Road through the common to Churchyard Bottom Wood (now Queen's Wood) where a footpath took you through the woods to Hornsey. During the nineteenth century several houses were built along Wood Lane and, in about 1900, Queen's Wood Road and Wood Vale replaced the Queen's Wood footpath, thus providing a continuous roadway from Highgate to Crouch End.

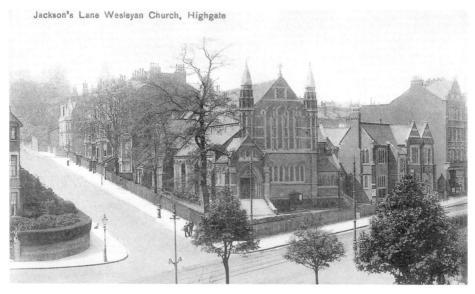

Highgate Wesleyan Methodist New Church (built in 1905), fronting Archway Road at the Jackson's Lane junction, *c.* 1906. W.H. Boney designed it in an early Gothic style. The church closed in about 1976 and work began converting it into Jackson's Lane Community Centre. Since then, it has become a well-known multi-arts community centre, but lack of capital investment left it in a state of neglect for many years. However, the centre has recently reopened following repairs and refurbishment work done in 2007.

View from Hornsey Lane Bridge of Archway Road facing north, c. 1910. St Augustine's Church, just a short way up on the right, is not yet visible as building work has not yet been completed on its Archway Road façade.

Archway Road facing south, c. 1933. St Augustine's Church is on the left of the picture, at the corner of Langdon Park Road and Archway Road. John Sedding designed the church in 1884 and Baroness Burdett-Coutts laid the foundation stone in 1887. Although the church was consecrated on 4 February 1888, due to financial restraints, it took many more years for the full structure to be completed. The nave wasn't completed until 1896 and the façade on Archway Road was only fully completed in 1913. Sadly, most of the church interior was destroyed by fire in January 1924. J. Harold Gibbons undertook the restoration work, which was completed in October 1925.

Archway Road looking south, near Tile Kiln Lane on the right, *c.* 1980. This early morning view completely disguises a usually busy stretch of road.

Langdon Park Lawn Tennis Club.

❖

5, *Langdon Park Road,*

*Highgate, N.*

*Nov 1st* ............189 1

*Dear Sir,*

*A Meeting of the Committee will be* held at *Mr J C Hill's The Newk,* *Whitehall Park* on *Friday* the *6th* inst at *8* p.m. Business *Re Drawing & Lengthening of Courts.*

*Your attendance is particularly requested.*

**W. H. WRIGHT,**

*Hon. Sec.*

*R W Stevenson Esq.*

Langdon Park Lawn Tennis Club, notice of a forthcoming committee meeting, 1891.

Gladsmuir Road, seen here in about 1905, with its large red-brick family houses, was built as part of the Whitehall Park Estate, designed by R.W. Hill in about 1889, with Whitehall Park and Gladsmuir Road being completed in 1891.

Whitehall Park, seen here in about 1914, was completed in 1891. The hillside road was designed with many grand houses for well-to-do families with live-in servants. Many kitchens came complete with a dumb-waiter, and a set of call-bells to summon servants.

St Andrew's Anglican Church (opened around 1895), Whitehall Park, at the junction of Whitehall Park and Gladsmuir Road, *c.* 1905. One of many new churches built in Islington during the late nineteenth century to cater for the ever-increasing population.

Harberton Road (seen here in about 1905), part of the Whitehall Park Estate, was completed in 1893. The surrounding roads now form the Whitehall Park Conservation Area, considered to be of special architectural or historic interest, the character or appearance of which it is desirable to preserve or enhance.

# 7

# *Highgate Archway*

The Old Highgate Archway, *c.* 1885. Archway Road was built in 1812–19 as a bypass (toll road) to the busy steep gradient of Highgate Hill and the narrow roads of Highgate Village. The original bypass plan included a tunnel to go under Hornsey Lane, but the tunnel collapsed several times during construction and it was then decided, on the recommendation of the eminent engineer John Rennie, to make a large cutting in the hill and to construct a brick-and-stone-built viaduct to carry the ancient Hornsey Lane over the new road. In 1812, John Nash designed the first Hornsey Lane Bridge, also called Highgate Archway, which opened in 1813, just a little bit north of where the present bridge stands.

This drawing by W. West shows the pedestrian footway that went through the west side of the old Highgate Archway, *c.* 1880.

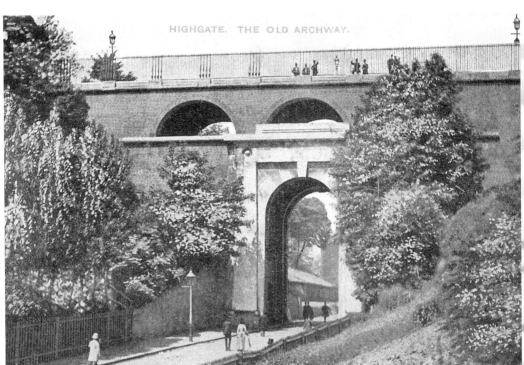

The Old Highgate Archway, *c.* 1885. The 7ft railings replaced the original brick balustrade and stone parapet in an attempt to prevent further suicides. Most people were still walking up Archway Road because the only available transport in this part of Highgate was horse-drawn, which was expensive. The Old Archway was too narrow for trams to use Archway Road.

The Old and New Highgate Archways, *c.* 1900. This view is facing north and shows the new Hornsey Lane Bridge and the Old Highgate Archway just a little way beyond it. The Old Archway is surrounded with scaffolding and is in the process of being demolished.

The new Highgate Archway, *c.* 1904. The new wide-span steel and cast-iron bridge was designed by London County Council's Chief Engineer, Sir Alexander Binnie, and opened on 28 July 1900. In this picture, the cutting's new retaining walls are in place, and new pavement and road surfaces are evident. The plaque in the centre of the bridge is dated 1897 to mark Queen Victoria's Diamond Jubilee and has no relevance to the bridge.

Electric tram beneath the Highgate Archway, *c*. 1905. The new bridge meant that electric trams could now pass through the arch. The Metropolitan Electric Tramways Co. started a tram service along Archway Road in 1905. This meant that public transport was now more affordable in this area of Highgate.

Highgate Archway over the Archway Road, looking south, *c*. 1905. This busy street scene shows a no. 104 tram passing under the archway. On the left of the picture is a busker playing an accordion, and on the right are a Findlaters' horse-drawn delivery cart and a Spiers & Pond Stores' delivery cart. Highgate Archway is known locally as Archway Bridge, Hornsey Lane Bridge and Suicide Bridge (a name favoured by the boys of St Aloysius' College, having an elevated view of it from Hornsey Lane).

Highgate Archway, looking up Archway Road to the north, *c.* 1905. Horse-drawn buses and carts compete against the new electric trams. At the time, people complained that the trams were noisy and caused congestion, but people using Archway Road today wouldn't mind too much if the level of congestion was like this!

Highgate Archway, looking up Archway Road to the north, *c.* 1912. Motorised buses had started to appear in 1908 and were now competing with the electric trams. By now, public transport was providing a good service from Highgate into central London. On the right of the picture, in between the advertising hoardings, are the steep steps leading up to the Hornsey Lane Bridge.

This War Memorial (seen here in 2008) was erected to honour the Aloysians (boys of St Aloysius' College) 'who gave their lives for their country in the Great War, 1914–18.' Further commemorative inscriptions were added to the memorial following the Second World War (1939–45). There are plaques at each side of the memorial listing the names of those who had died in each war. The memorial is situated between the college and the bridge on Hornsey Lane, opposite Tile Kiln Lane.

# 8

# *Hampstead Heath*

680   HAMPSTEAD HEATH. — *White Stone Pond*, — LL.

Whitestone Pond, *c.* 1905. Hampstead Heath borders the west side of Highgate and is London's largest ancient parkland with over twenty-five ponds spread out across 791 acres (320 hectares) of rambling unspoiled countryside. Whitestone Pond is situated at the highest natural point in London, 440ft (134m) above sea level, on the west side of the Heath at the junction of West Heath Road and Heath Street. It was originally a small dew-pond called the Horse Pond, a name it acquired because riders on the Heath would wash and cool their horses' legs in its waters. It owes its present name to a nearby white milestone, which indicates 4 miles from St Giles' Pound, near to Holborn in London. Whitestone Pond was believed to be the first stretch of water near London to freeze in winter and provide ice-skating.

Jack Straw's Castle and War Memorial in the1920s, situated on the west side of the Heath at the junction of Heath Street and Spaniards Road, near to Whitestone Pond. Originally built as a coaching inn in 1781, it was named after Jack Straw, a comrade of Wat Tyler who was the leader of the 1381 Peasants' Revolt against King Richard II. Jack Straw was said to have addressed groups of peasants on Hampstead Heath from a hay wagon, which was known as Jack Straw's Castle.

Jack Straw's Castle, *c.* 1920s. The building was repaired following bomb damage it suffered in the Second World War and it was completely rebuilt in 1962–64. This huge three-storey pub looks very different today with its much-admired 1960s mock-castle elevations. Now a Grade II listed building, it has recently been converted into luxury apartments.

The Vale of Health as viewed from Jack Straw's Castle, *c.* 1905. This was originally known as Hatch's Bottom after Samuel Hatch, a harness maker who built the first cottage there in about 1720 on what was then bog land next to a small pond. In 1777, the Hampstead Water Co. enlarged the Vale's pond, drained the marshy ground and three cottages were built there for the poor.

The Vale of Health, *c.* 1905. By 1851, the hamlet had grown from four poor cottages to eighteen houses, of which five were large houses used as country retreats by the gentry. The Vale became increasingly desirable, especially after the opening of the Hampstead Heath railway station in 1860.

Vale of Health Hotel and pond, *c.* 1904. The Vale of Health Hotel (built around 1863), formerly known as the Hampstead Heath Hotel and the Vale of Health Tavern. In about 1900, the failing hotel converted rooms upstairs into studios. It was in his studio there in 1914 that Henry Lamb (1883–1960) painted the portrait of Lytton Strachey (now in the Tate Gallery). Spencer House Flats, named after Stanley Spencer who shared Henry Lamb's studio, replaced the Vale of Health Hotel in 1964.

314  Bank holiday on Hampstead Heath.

Londoners enjoy a bank holiday on Hampstead Heath. *c.* 1905. The fairground site by the Vale of Health was very popular with visiting families, but the rowdiness was not so popular with locals.

Strollers enjoy the Sunday sunshine along the Spaniards Road, *c.* 1912.

Bank holiday on Hampstead Heath by the Willow Road coffee stall, *c.* 1905. Since the opening of Hampstead Heath railway station in 1860, the Heath had become known as the playground for London's East Enders on their rare days off work. 'Appy 'Ampstead became a nationally known phrase in the 1890s when the Heath would attract more than 100,000 visitors on bank holidays. By 1910, the crowds became enormous, with a reported 200,000 on Easter Monday (always the Heath's busiest day).

View of Hampstead Heath from the viaduct, in the middle of Hampstead Heath, *c.* 1905. The viaduct was designed by Joseph Gwilt and built in about 1845 for Sir Thomas Maryon Wilson (1800–1869). Sir Thomas inherited around 240 acres of Hampstead Heath from his father, but he was restricted to issuing twenty-one-year leases on the land. Sir Thomas wanted to exploit the land and planned to build twenty-eight luxury villas on it. He started to build an access road from Jack Straw's Castle to Downshire Hill and he built the viaduct to cross the swampy marsh valley in the middle. However, his plans were thwarted when he fought and lost a long parliamentary battle to obtain power of enclosure on the Heath. The villas had still not been built when he died in 1869 and the viaduct then earned the nickname of 'Wilson's Folly'. The swampy valley was later drained to form an ornamental pond. The viaduct is now a Grade II listed building and is used as part of the Heath's cycle track. The Metropolitan Board of Works purchased this part of the Heath from Sir Thomas Wilson's heirs following his death in 1869 and the Hampstead Heath Act of 1871 was put in place to protect the Heath's future.

*Opposite bottom:* A happy group of young people enjoying a day out on Hampstead Heath, *c.* 1905.

*Above:* The viaduct, *c.* 1905. Hampstead Heath was taken over and managed by the London County Council (LCC) from 1899 until 1972 when the Greater London Council (GLC) replaced the LCC. In 1978, the Heath and Old Hampstead Society were formed to further protect the Heath. In 1986, the GLC was abolished and responsibility for the Heath was transferred to the London Residuary Body. In 1989, the Corporation of London was formed and took over the management of Hampstead Heath, except for 112 acres (45 hectares) at Kenwood, which are maintained by English Heritage.

316 A Happy Group on Hampstead Heath.

*Above:* Golders Hill House, seen here in about 1908, was built as a private house in the late eighteenth century. Its last private occupant was Sir Thomas Spencer Wells (1818–1897), surgeon to Queen Victoria's household and president of the Royal College of Surgeons. In 1875, he had the house enlarged to the designs of E.F. Clarke. After his death in 1897, the house and its grounds were acquired by the London County Council for use as a public park for the people of London. A Second World War bomb destroyed the house in 1941. Golders Hill Park is adjacent to Hampstead West Heath but is not part of the Heath.

The Bull and Bush in North End Way, Hampstead, seen here in about 1906, is one of London's oldest and most famous pubs. Now a Grade II listed building, it stands on the site of a farmhouse that was built in about 1645 during the reign of Charles I. Records show that the farmhouse obtained a licence to sell ale in 1721. The pub's name was supposedly contrived from the bull of the farm and the bush was a yew tree that is said to have been planted by the London born artist William Hogarth (1697–1764). Hogarth was a regular drinker at the Old Bull and Bush, and apparently often stayed at the inn during summer months. He is said to have sat drinking ale here while painting at least one in the series of his 'Rake's Progress' paintings. Several other eighteenth-century English painters were attracted to the area by the magnificent local views. These included Thomas Gainsborough and Joshua Reynolds who were both regular drinkers at the Old Bull and Bush. It was also a haunt and source of inspiration for many literary scholars and thespians, including the Shakespearian actor David Garrick, who had his portrait painted by both Hogarth and Gainsborough.

*Opposite, bottom:* Wylde's Farm, North End, Hampstead Heath, seen here in about 1904, was formerly know as Collin's Farm after the former farm owner. William Blake (1757–1827), English artist and poet, used to lodge here and John Linnell (1792–1882), English landscape painter, lived here in about 1824. The farmland was bought by the London County Council and added to Hampstead Heath in 1907.

The Bull and Bush, North End Way *c.* 1905. The Bull and Bush obtained its first music licence in 1867, and quickly became a popular venue for London's East Enders to visit while on their day trips to the countryside. By the end of the nineteenth century, it was renowned for its lovely gardens and musical entertainment, with famous outdoor concerts and singsongs, often accompanied by four or five piece German bands.

The Bull and Bush entertainers practise their act on the garden entertainment stage, *c.* 1903. The singsong tradition continued well into the twentieth century, and it was about 1910 when singer Florrie Ford (1875–1940) made the pub world famous with her music hall rendition of the song 'Down at the Old Bull and Bush', which is reputed to have been written in the pub's garden.

Cosy nooks at the Bull and Bush, *c.* 1904. Much of the pub building was reconstructed in 1924, when part of the old garden was made into a car park. It was refurbished in 1987 and again in 2006. When it reopened to the public on 24 March 2006, following its latest refurbishment, it became one of the first completely smoke-free pubs in London. The overall smoking ban in English pubs became law on 1 July 2007. The pub also lends its name to the only London underground station that never even opened. The disused station, originally named North End but nicknamed Bull and Bush by London Underground staff, is situated between Hampstead and Golders Green on the Northern Line. It was planned to be the deepest underground station on the whole Underground network at 200ft below ground level, and intended to be opened in 1907 when the line was extended through to Golders Green. However, due to planning restrictions covering the local conservation area, the building work was abandoned and the station never opened. The unused station platforms can still be seen when travelling southbound on the Northern Line train between Golders Green and Hampstead.

The Spaniard's Inn, seen here in about 1908, is situated at the Highgate end of Spaniards Road. The inn stands on the site of a lodge once occupied by the keeper of the ancient tollgate on the right. This gate formed one of the entrances to the then Bishop of London's park. There is no certainty as to how the inn came by its name, but rumour has is that it was built in 1585 as the country house of the Spanish ambassador. Dickens often drank here and he featured the inn in *The Pickwick Papers* (1836) and *Barnaby Rudge* (1841). The poet John Keats (1795–1821) also frequented the inn while he lived in Hampstead (*c*. 1818). It is yet another inn where Dick Turpin, the famous highwayman, is said to have stabled his horses.

An organ player entertains visitors to the Hampstead Heath, *c*. 1908.

# 9

# *Highgate's Neighbours*

High Street, Hampstead, *c.* 1905. A horse-drawn bus passes the King of Bohemia pub and the Hampstead Brewery, which was established by the then owner of Jack Straw's Castle in 1720. The frontage of the brewery was rebuilt in 1869 and by 1928 it employed 184 people. The brewery closed in 1932 and the refurbished building is a now flats with shops to the ground floor.

Finchley Road, Hampstead, seen here in about 1908, was built in the late 1820s and early 1830s as a turnpike road, with a tollgate at Childs Hill near to the junction of Cricklewood Lane. Built to link London's West End with the Great North Road, it runs from St John's Wood through West Hampstead and up to Hampstead Garden Suburb at the junction of the North Circular Road. After its construction, many grand houses were built along its length and it became a heavily used route in and out of London. Development continued throughout the nineteenth and twentieth centuries, making it the densely populated road it is today.

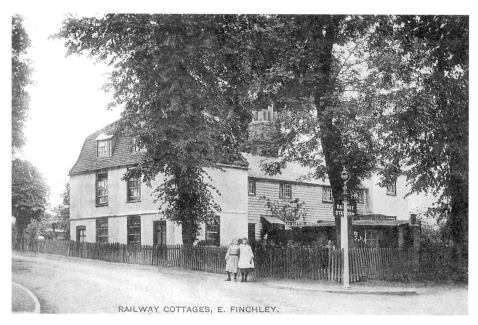

RAILWAY COTTAGES, E. FINCHLEY.

Railway Cottages, East Finchley, *c.* 1905. In 1867, the Great Northern Railway opened East End Finchley station, but local residents did not like the name, which they thought suggested a link with London's East End. In 1886, the name was changed to East Finchley station.

High Road, East Finchley, *c.* 1908. The land on which East Finchley now stands was once part of the Bishop of London's hunting ground. Travellers using the then countryside route between Market Place and King's Street were made to pay a toll from about 1712 until about 1862; the tollgate was removed in 1901. The opening of East Finchley station in 1867 caused the shopping district to shift from the market area to the High Road.

The Market Place, East Finchley, *c.* 1904. In the sixteenth and seventeenth centuries, Market Place, at the then centre of the village, was a well-known pig market. By the eighteenth century it had become the largest pig market in Middlesex and was known as the Hogmarket. By the late nineteenth century, the pig market was in decline with most of the remaining trade taking place outside the eighteenth-century George Inn. The George Inn was rebuilt in the 1890s and was demolished in March 2001.

Queen's Parade, Muswell Hill, *c*. 1909. In 1896, James Edmondson bought up 30 acres of flat land at the centre of the village with the intention of developing good quality shops and large family houses for people working in central London. Queen's Parade was the first of the Muswell Hill shopping parades built by James Edmondson in 1897. Muswell Hill Village is named after an ancient mossy spring that was situated on Muswell Road.

The Exchange, Muswell Hill, *c*. 1903. James Edmondson started building The Exchange shopping parades in 1900 and, in September 1901, Parke's Drug Stores opened for business at the newly-built no. 12 The Exchange. Ainslie's Family Butcher's and J. Sainsbury are on the right of the picture, with Muswell Hill Baptist Church in the centre and the Union Bank of London immediately to the right of Parke's.

Alexandra Park Road, Muswell Hill, *c.* 1908. The area was laid out over former Rhodes farmland in 1891, but development didn't really begin until about 1900. St Andrew's Church (built in about 1903) is in the distance at the junction of Windermere Road. The London Parcels Delivery Co. (which merged with Pickfords in 1912) can be seen here delivering by horse and cart to one of the newly-built houses.

Crouch End Playing Fields, situated west of Park Road, with a view of Alexandra Palace on the hill in the distance, *c.* 1905. Alexandra Palace was rebuilt by architect John Johnson and reopened in 1875 after the original building had burnt down just a few days after it opened in 1873. The world's first public television broadcast, by the BBC, took place here in 1936. It was again restored and reopened in 1988 following a fire in 1980.

The Green Man, Muswell Hill, *c.* 1904. This early nineteenth-century building with its late nineteenth-century hotel extension is thought to have originated from a sixteenth-century stone-built alehouse recorded as having been on Muswell Hill in about 1552. The front elevations of the building look very different today but the original outline can just about be recognised. To the right of the pub is Muswell Hill station (built 1873) which closed down in 1956 and is now occupied by Muswell Hill Primary School.

BROADWAY CROUCH END.

Crouch End Broadway, *c.* 1905. The red-brick clock tower in the middle of Crouch End Broadway was built in 1895 as a memorial to Henry Reader Williams (1822–1897) in recognition of public services rendered by him, including helping to save Highgate Woods from development. The Topsfield Parade of shops was built in 1895 by James Edmondson on the site of the ancient Topsfield Manor between Middle Lane and Tottenham Lane.

The Three Compasses pub in Hornsey High Street, *c.* 1880. This eighteenth-century pub was demolished in about 1896 and a three-storey terrace of shops was erected to include a rebuilt pub of the same name.

Hornsey Rise, with Upper Hornsey Rise (now Hillrise Road) on the right, *c.* 1913. The building on the right is the Hornsey Rise High School for Boys. The sight of a motorcar captivates onlookers, but the modern world is approaching fast with advertising posters displayed all along the fence at the side of the road.

Highgate Road, Kentish Town, looking south towards Kentish Town Road with St John's Church on the right, *c.* 1909. Kentish Town is recorded as far back as the thirteenth century (*kentisston*), and by the fifteenth century it was a thriving rural village nestled on the edge of the now submerged river Fleet. The area underwent large-scale development during the nineteenth and twentieth centuries, and today there are no visible remains of its ancient buildings. Kentish Town is now a fully urbanised suburb of London; its rural character has long disappeared.

The Boston Hotel, Junction Road, Tufnell Park, 1906. This pub was originally called the Boston Arms Tavern when it first opened in 1860. It underwent extensive rebuilding work in 1899 and was repaired and refurbished in 1968 following a fire. The pub is now known as the Boston Arms and it boasts multi-screen sport, live music and a nightclub. It stands opposite Tufnell Park underground station, which was in the process of being built when this photograph was taken; it was subsequently opened in 1907.

Tufnell Park Road, with St George's Church (built in about 1865) on the right at the junction of Carleton Road, c. 1908. The circular church was designed by George Truffit and was said to have been based a fifth-century Greek church and also modelled on Shakespeare's Globe Theatre. It fell into disuse in the 1960s and was used as an Elizabethan theatre in the 1970s under the name St George's Theatre. In 2004, the building was taken over by a group of squatters. The Grade II listed building is currently being renovated for use as a church again.

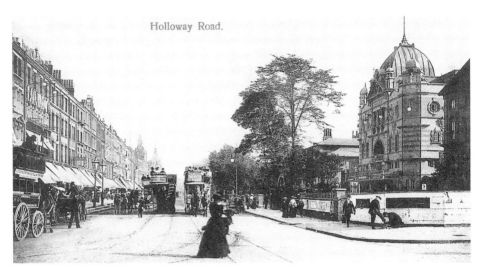

Holloway Road.

Holloway Road at the junction of Parkhurst Road, with the famous Marlborough Theatre on the right, *c.* 1906. This magnificent theatre was designed by theatre architect Frank Matcham for owner Frederick William Purcell. It opened on 5 October 1903 and was successful for several years, presenting opera, plays and musical comedies. It began showing films in 1907 and was refurbished as a cinema (Marlborough Picture Theatre) in 1918. It closed in 1957 and was demolished in 1962. City & Islington College now occupy the site in a tower block known as the Marlborough Building.

St. John's Church, Upper Holloway.

St John's Church at the junction of Holloway Road and Pemberton Gardens, Upper Holloway, *c.* 1906. The church was built around 1826–1828 from the designs of Sir Charles Barry. In the nineteenth century, the church had an Orphan's Room in the gallery where children from the local workhouse could be taken to hear the services but not be seen. This Anglican church is still in use today.

# INDEX